Beyond Team Building

Beyond Team Building

How to Build High Performing Teams and the Culture to Support Them

Gibb Dyer

Jeff Dyer

WILEY

Published by John Wiley & Sons, Inc., Hoboken, New Jersey.

Published simultaneously in Canada.

For general information on our other products and services or for technical support, please contact our Customer Care Department within the United States at (800) 762–2974, outside the United States at (317) 572–3993 or fax (317) 572–4002.

Wiley publishes in a variety of print and electronic formats and by print-on-demand. Some material included with standard print versions of this book may not be included in e-books or in print-on-demand. If this book refers to media such as a CD or DVD that is not included in the version you purchased, you may download this material at http://booksupport.wiley.com. For more information about Wiley products, visit www.wiley.com.

Library of Congress Cataloging-in-Publication Data

Names: Dyer, Gibb, Jr., 1954- author. | Dyer, Jeff, author.
Title: Beyond team building : how to build high performing teams and the
  culture to support them / W. Gibb Dyer and Jeffrey H. Dyer.
Description: First Edition. | Hoboken : Wiley, [2020] | Includes index. |
  Identifiers: LCCN 2019005900 (print) | LCCN 2019007093 (ebook) | ISBN
  9781119551386 (ePub) | ISBN 9781119551393 (ePDF) | ISBN 9781119551409
  (hardcover)
Subjects: LCSH: Teams in the workplace. | Teams in the workplace—Management.
  | Leadership.
Classification: LCC HD66 (ebook) | LCC HD66 .D943 2020 (print) | DDC
  658.4/022—dc23
LC record available at https://lccn.loc.gov/2019005900

Cover Design: Wiley
Cover Image: © Artistdesign29/Shutterstock

Printed in the United States of America

V10012695_080219

To our father, Bill Dyer, the father of Team Building.

Contents

Acknowledgments

We would like to thank Natalia Smith, Emily Powers, and the staff at Wiley for their help in gathering data and editing this book. Their work has made this book immeasurably better. The secretaries in the management department, Sophie S. Poulsen, Kesley B. Powell, and Katy Milagro Nottingham, went the extra mile to ensure that the tables and figures in the book are accurate.

About the Authors

Gibb Dyer (Ph.D MIT) is the O. Leslie Stone Professor of Entrepreneurship and Management in the Marriott School of Business at Brigham Young University. He has been a visiting faculty member at the University of New Hampshire and IESE in Barcelona, Spain, and a visiting scholar at the University of Bath in the U.K. He has published nine books and over 50 articles and his research has been featured in publications such as *Fortune*, the *Wall Street Journal*, and the *New York Times*. His most recent book, titled *The Family Edge*, focuses on how families and family teams support business growth. He has been ranked as one of the top-ten scholars in the world in the field of family business. His consulting practice focuses on team building, organization development, and management succession.

Jeff Dyer (Ph.D UCLA) is the Horace Beesley Distinguished Professor of Strategy at BYU and the Wharton School, University of Pennsylvania. He worked previously as a management consultant at Bain & Company and cofounded the Innovator's DNA consultancy. He is the author of two bestsellers, *The Innovator's DNA* and *The Innovator's Method*. Among those receiving Ph.Ds after 1990 he was ranked #1 Most Influential Scholar with over 35,000 citations and over 500,000 Google searches to his name.

INTRODUCTION

To me, teamwork is the beauty of our sport, where you have five acting as one.
You become selfless.

—Duke Coach Mike Krzyzewski

Teamwork is the hallmark of success in sports and in business. As Ken Blanchard once wrote: "None of us is as smart as all of us." Many books on teams and teamwork (including our own) focus on how to repair broken teams in which team members are not "acting as one." But this book has a different purpose. We go beyond focusing on how to repair broken teams, and focus on how to create a "team building organization" that will foster an environment which will create and maintain great teams from the outset. (Duke Coach Mike Krzyzewski's success is based on creating a set of processes and an environment that produces great teams from the outset, not just on fixing his teams when they aren't performing well.) And while we cover many topics from our previous books on team building, this book will give to you, the reader, a more succinct and clear description of how to create an effective team. You will also learn how to develop a "team building organization" that has systems and processes in place to regularly assess team performance for all teams in the organization and to help them improve. To do so, we take a broader view about what team building is and should mean for managers, team leaders, and team members.

This book is for anyone interested in improving team performance. While most of our examples are from teams in businesses, the team building techniques we describe can be used to help

1

families, teams in nonprofit organizations, civic or governmental teams, sports teams, or almost any type of team that you can imagine. The book is especially designed to help organizational leaders and managers understand their roles in helping teams succeed. Team leaders and team members will find our diagnostic models and interventions particularly helpful as they try to make their teams more effective. Human resource managers, who are often assigned to help teams improve, will be aided by this book, as will team consultants and team facilitators whose roles are to improve and strengthen teams.

A Brief History of Team Building

The theories behind what makes an effective team came out of the T-group movement (the T stood for "training"), which in the 1960s was largely sponsored by National Training Laboratories. The assumption underlying the T-group was that individuals—and particularly organizational leaders—were impaired by the assumptions and authoritarian, top-down style that management held about their subordinates and coworkers. The T-group was designed to help change those assumptions and to make managers more trusting, open, and participative as they worked with others. In the 1960s, many organizations that wanted to use the T-group to improve the performance of their leaders and those within the "T-group movement" really believed in the T-group as the vehicle to change the world of work by changing the values of organization leaders. By changing top management's values, these new values would eventually filter down throughout the organization to effect organization-wide change and transform the organization into having more humane and creative systems.

However, a 1968 study conducted by two academics, John Campbell and Marvin Dunnette, changed most of that thinking.[1] Campbell and Dunnette reviewed the major studies that had looked at the impact of T-group training on individuals and on organizations and concluded that:

> [Our] examination of the research literature leads to the conclusion
> that while T-group training seems to produce observable changes
> in behavior, the utility of these changes for the performance of
> individuals in their organizational roles remains to be demonstrated.[2]

Campbell and Dunnette reported that the T-group did in fact help individuals become more comfortable with themselves and their ability to manage interpersonal relationships. However, their review also showed that T-group training had virtually no impact (and sometimes a negative effect) on team and organizational performance. The T-group experience often helped people become more open and honest, but this sometimes also led to dysfunctional confrontations and didn't actually solve the team's specific performance problems.

Given these findings, T-group trainers, such as our father, Bill Dyer, made a decision regarding their work. Bill and others decided to create a new paradigm for working with groups—the team building paradigm. Bill wrote about this change from T-groups to team building as follows:

> As practitioners developed more experience in applying the T-group
> methods to work units, the T-group mode shifted to take into
> account the differences of the new setting. It became clear that the
> need was not just to let people get feedback, but to help the work
> unit develop into a more effective, collaborative, problem-solving
> unit with work to get out and goals to achieve. Slowly, the
> methodology shifted from the unstructured T-group to a more
> focused, defined process of training a group of interdependent people
> in collaborative work and problem-solving procedures.[3]

Bill worked as consultant to many teams facing problems, and in 1977, he published the first book on team building that captured the essence of his consulting experience and his model for helping teams become more effective. The book was an instant success because the theories, methods, and exercises he described in the book were built on real-world experience and they worked. These proved invaluable to managers, team leaders, and consultants. Over the years, Bill added new material to keep up with the changing times and the evolution of the field. After he passed away in 1997, we continued this tradition of helping teams to be more effective.

Beyond Team Building: What's in It for You?

In *Beyond Team Building* we explain our 4C model of team performance and expand it to add an additional C—*collaborative leadership*. Team leadership has been somewhat neglected in our previous writings, so we will emphasize it here. Furthermore, we show how to apply the new "5C" model to a variety of different teams—entrepreneurial, family, alliance, temporary, cross-cultural, and virtual teams—teams that are becoming increasingly important. Some cases, such virtual teams, were unheard of when Bill developed his team building approach in the 1970s. Today, teams are more diverse, are more agile, and are more geographically separated. This is largely due to the new demands of a global economy, and reflects the need for today's teams to respond more quickly to changes in the marketplace. Furthermore, we've discovered that for most companies to become successful, they will need to become "team building organizations" where team development becomes ingrained in the day-to-day activities of the organization. While some people tend to think of team building as simply a fun team activity, such as river rafting or having the team go together through a "ropes course" to conquer certain physical and mental challenges, we view these activities as only part of team development. By themselves these activities are unlikely to make a difference in team performance in the workplace.

The book is structured as follows, the first six chapters present our 5C model of team performance and share various diagnostic surveys to help you assess how a team is doing along these dimensions. Each chapter provides guidance on what a team needs in order to perform well on that particular dimension. Chapter 7 will help you see how to bring the 5Cs together to create an effective team building program, while Chapter 8 describes the key team building interventions that we use to initiate change in a team. Chapters 9 and 10 are devoted to explaining how the 5C model can be applied to temporary teams, cross-cultural teams, virtual teams, alliance teams, entrepreneurial teams, and family teams. These teams are quite different from each other and require different approaches to applying the 5C model. Chapter 11 demonstrates how to create a "team building organization" by using Cisco Systems as an example of an organization that has attempted to make its teams and team development a priority. With this overview in mind, let's begin our journey to help our teams be more effective.

Notes

1. J. Campbell and M. Dunnette, "Effectiveness of T-Group Experiences in Managerial Training and Development," *Psychological Bulletin* 70 (1968): 73–103.
2. Ibid., p. 73.
3. W. Dyer, *Team Building: Issues and Alternatives* (Reading, MA: Addison-Wesley, 1977), 23.

THE FIVE CS OF TEAM PERFORMANCE

Albert Einstein once said: "What a person does on his own, without being stimulated by the thoughts and experiences of others, is even in the best of cases rather paltry and monotonous." Einstein was simply recognizing that producing great things—whether it be new products, services, internal processes—requires the collective efforts of a team. Leaders of highly successful companies understand that business is a team sport—and they work to build an organization comprised of effective work teams.

As we begin our study of teams and team performance, you might start by thinking about your previous team experiences. Think about each team: How did that team perform and how did that team affect you as a member of the team? While we might not think of it as a team, the first "team" that we were a part of is our family. In a family we learn whether we can trust other people, how to work (or not work) together, how to help one another, how to communicate, and how to solve problems. Our family team is not one that we can typically choose—it's a function of fate—but nevertheless it has a significant impact on how we think about working together in a group setting and how to function effectively in a team. As we age and go to school we begin to function in other types of teams: sports teams, debate teams, study-groups, musical groups, and so forth. From our experience in these teams, we also develop our attitudes about whether we like being on a team and whether we feel that being a part of a team will help us achieve our goals.

After our schooling (and oftentimes during our years in school) we begin to experience what it's like to be on a work team within an organization. Whether it's a team preparing fast-food, managing inventory, developing new products, or even hoping to cure cancer, we bring our experiences from the teams of our youth and they influence us as we become a part of these work teams. Unfortunately, in today's world, many people have not had particularly positive experiences on teams: their "family team" didn't function particularly well, their sports teams had poor coaching leading to low morale and losses, or their study-groups ended up producing a poor product (and a poor grade), making them leery of being part of a team. Indeed, much of the current research on Millennials suggests that they don't particularly enjoy being part of a team, and don't have many of the skills needed for effective teamwork.[1] One of the interesting findings from our research is that while many organizations give lip service to the importance of teams, few spend time or resources to ensure the effective performance of their teams.[2] The typical excuses we hear are:

- We don't have time to spend "working on our team." We've got more important work to do.

- Management doesn't reward good team performance. Individual performance is what matters.

- If we start looking at what is going on in our team, people will be uncomfortable. We don't believe a "touchy-feely" approach will lead to good outcomes for the team.

- Our team leaders don't really know how to develop an effective team, and we don't have the expertise internally to train them all. And outside consultants are too expensive.

The result of these types of attitudes is that little effort is generally made to improve team performance in today's organizations, and the efforts that are made are typically one-time training or other "band-aid" approaches to helping teams perform more effectively.

The net result is that we have many dysfunctional teams today, and not much is being done to make them better.

Even though often little is done to improve teams, leaders are generally aware that team performance is important as much of today's work is team based; think of research teams, product development teams, production teams, sales and marketing teams, cross-functional problem-solving teams, and top management teams. One reason work is done more by teams now is that products and services have become increasingly complex, requiring a wide range of skills and technologies. No single person is capable of developing, manufacturing, and selling increasingly complex products, which means that teams of individuals with complementary knowledge must coordinate efficiently and effectively in order to be successful. This requires teamwork skills. A second reason teamwork skills are needed now more than in the past is that in a global economy, individuals must collaborate across cultural, organizational, and geographical boundaries to accomplish their goals. Hence, the need for cross-cultural, virtual, and alliance teams (teams that collaborate across organizational boundaries) has increased in recent years. Thus, high-performing companies in today's competitive landscape essentially require high-performing work teams. The two unavoidably go hand in hand.

High-performing teams are those with members whose skills, attitudes, and competencies enable them to achieve team goals. These team members set goals, make decisions, communicate, manage conflict, and solve problems in a supportive, trusting atmosphere in order to accomplish their objectives. Moreover, they are aware of their own strengths and weaknesses and have the ability to make changes when they need to improve their performance.

Thus, the primary purpose of this book is to give managers, team leaders, team members, and team consultants specific guidance on how to improve team performance. In particular, this book gives you "the essentials" of team building—those activities and actions that can help poorly performing or dysfunctional teams improve their performance. And for those who have adequately functioning teams, this book can help you transform them into great teams.

Determinants of High-Performing Teams: The Five Cs

Over the past several decades, as we have consulted with teams and conducted research on team performance, we have come to the conclusion that five factors—the Five Cs—must be understood and managed for teams to achieve superior performance (Figure 1.1):

1. Context for the team
2. Composition of the team
3. Competencies of the team
4. Change management skills of the team
5. Collaborative leadership style

Figure 1.1 The Five Cs of Team Performance

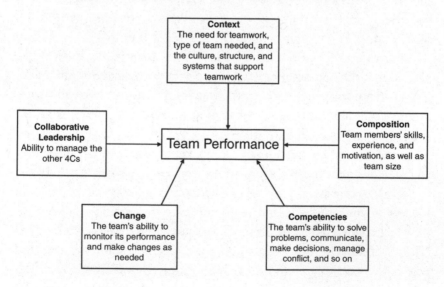

We will describe each of these factors only briefly here. Future chapters are devoted to each one of the 5Cs.

Context for the Team

Team context refers to the organizational environment in which the team must work. Understanding context, and how it influences team performance, requires an understanding of the answers to the following two categories of questions:

1. Is effective teamwork critical to accomplishing organizational goals? If so, are there measurable team performance goals around which we can organize a team?

2. Do the following support teamwork in the organization?
    - Senior management—Do they encourage teamwork?
    - Reward systems—Is teamwork rewarded with financial or other rewards?
    - Information systems—Do we have data on team performance that teams can access?
    - Structure—Are teams organized in a way that allows the team to accomplish their goals?
    - Culture—Do members of the organization value teamwork?
    - Physical space—Are there spaces for teams to meet so they can accomplish their work effectively?

Experience has shown that teamwork skills are more important when the team must complete a complex task characterized by a high degree of interdependence between team members. Understanding the context—the nature of task interdependence required among team members in order to achieve a high level of performance—is a critical first step to building a successful team. For example, it's not enough just to train people on the importance of key team competencies, such as communication and problem solving, if they are not supported and reinforced by the specific context of the team. Low-interdependence teams need to be managed differently than high-interdependence teams.

Composition of the Team

The composition of the team concerns the skills and attitudes of each team member. You must to have the right people on the team to achieve the desired level of performance. To effectively manage the composition of the team, those staffing the team must answer the following questions:

- Do individual team members have the technical skills required to complete the task?
- Do they have the interpersonal and communication skills required to coordinate their work with others? (This is much more important for teams where task interdependence is high.)
- Are individual team members committed to the team and motivated to complete the task?
- Is the team the right size to complete the task successfully?

Teams saddled with members who are not motivated to accomplish the task or lack the skills to achieve team goals are doomed to failure from the outset. Team composition also refers to assembling a group of individuals with complementary skills. Effective teams use the diverse skills and abilities of each team member in a synergistic way to achieve high performance. The members of high-performing teams clearly understand their roles and assignments and carry them out with commitment.

Team size also plays a significant role in team effectiveness. A team that is too large may be unwieldy and cause members to lose interest due to a lack of individual involvement. Amazon employs a "two-pizza team" philosophy, meaning that teams should be small enough (five to ten people) to be adequately fed by two pizzas.

Amazon finds that having small teams empowers team members and facilitates more effective coordination. However, having too few team members may place unnecessary burdens on individual team members, and the team may not have the resources needed to accomplish its goals.

High-performing teams manage team composition by (1) establishing processes to select individuals for the team who are both skilled and motivated, (2) establishing processes that develop the technical and interpersonal skills of individual team members as well as their commitment to achieving team goals, (3) removing those from the team who lack skills or motivation, and (4) ensuring that the team is the right size: a team that is neither too large nor too small to accomplish the task.

Competencies of the Team

We have found that successful teams have certain competencies that exist independent of any single member of the team. These competencies are embedded in the team's formal and informal processes—its way of functioning. High-performing teams have developed processes that allow the team to:

- Clearly articulate their goals and the metrics related to those goals.
- Clearly articulate the means required to achieve the goals, ensuring that individuals understand their assignments and how their work contributes to team goals.
- Make effective decisions.
- Hold individuals and the team accountable for performance.
- Organize and run effective meetings.
- Build trust and commitment to the team and its goals.
- Effectively communicate, including giving and receiving feedback.
- Resolve disputes or disagreements.

- Have mutual respect for one another.
- Encourage risk taking and innovation.

While the context and composition of the team set the stage, these competencies propel it to high performance. If the team hopes to be extraordinary, it must develop competencies for goal setting, decision making, communicating, trust building, dispute resolution, and so forth.

Change Management Skills of the Team

Effective teams must change and adapt to new conditions to be successful over time. Team context, composition, and competencies may need to change or be refocused for the team to succeed in reaching a new goal. A team that is able to monitor its performance and understand its strengths and weaknesses can generate insights needed to develop a plan of action to continually improve. Toyota, a company that we've researched extensively, uses the *kaizen*, or continuous-improvement, philosophy to help its teams identify the bottlenecks they are facing and then develop strategies to eliminate the bottlenecks.[3] Toyota's managers are never fully satisfied with their team's performance because once they've fixed one problem, they know that to continuously improve they need to find and fix the next one. We have found that teams in most companies, unlike Toyota, are oblivious to their weaknesses. And even when they do recognize them, they do not have the ability to manage change effectively to overcome those weaknesses. It is possible to view change management skills as just another team competency, but this meta-competency is so important that it deserves special attention. In Chapter 8 we describe the key interventions that are often used by teams to change how they function and by so doing improve their performance.

High-performing teams have developed the ability to change by (1) establishing team-building processes that result in the regular evaluation of team context, composition, competencies, and leadership with the explicit objective of initiating needed changes to better achieve the desired team goals, and (2) establishing a philosophy among team members that regular change is necessary to meet the demands of a constantly changing world.

Collaborative Leadership on the Team

The final C in our model is "collaborative leadership." Collaboration is the key to success for teams and team leaders. Team leaders are responsible for managing the other 4Cs of team performance. They must work with senior management and those responsible for creating the context factors, such as the reward system, to ensure that the team has the right environment to succeed. The team leader typically works with human resources or other managers to identify and assign members to his or her team and then provides for each team member's development.

While team leaders might be able to provide all the training needed regarding the competencies in the team, they will typically need support from others to provide this training. This is also true regarding the change management strategies that might be used by the team leader to improve the team. Hence, we see the effective team leader as someone who is a "boundary spanner"—someone who looks at the factors both inside and outside of the team and then garners the resources needed to help the team achieve its goals. In fact, we have created a ranking of the world's most innovative leaders that is published in *Forbes* (as the "Forbes 100 most innovative leaders list"), and the most important distinguishing feature of effective leaders is that they develop the capacity to bring resources to the team so that it can achieve its goals (see *Innovation Capital: How to Compete—and Win—Like the World's Most Innovative Leaders* by Jeff Dyer[4]).

Team leaders also need to recognize what type of leadership style the team needs in order to foster the appropriate type of collaboration with the leader and among team members. When team members are relatively inexperienced and need significant direction, leaders should use a more directive leadership style and follow up more closely with team members to collaborate with them in doing their work. In other instances, team leaders may have a team comprised of highly seasoned, trustworthy, and competent members. In that case, the team leader would likely play the role of a coach and allow the team to use a participative decision-making process. Team members could be given wider latitude in doing their jobs and would likely need much less direction. Leadership style is an important key to the success of the team leader. Thus, the organization needs to choose team leaders who (1) understand that their role is to manage the other 4Cs of team performance and collaboratively secure the resources needed to achieve team goals, and (2) are attuned to the maturity of their team so they can use the appropriate leadership style to get maximum motivation and performance from team members.

Notes

1. J. M. Twenge, W. K. Campbell, and E. C. Freeman, "Generational Differences in Young Adults' Life Goals, Concern for Others and Civic Orientation, 1966–2009," *Journal of Personality and Social Psychology* 102, no. 5 (2012): 1045–1062.
2. W. Dyer, J. Dyer, and W. Dyer, *Team Building*, 5th ed. (New York: Wiley, 2013).
3. Ibid.
4. J. H. Dyer (in press), *Innovation Capital: How to Compete—and Win—Like the World's Most Innovative Leaders* (Boston: Harvard Business Review Press).

2

CONTEXT: THE FOUNDATION OF TEAM EFFECTIVENESS

Several years ago, we were asked to consult with a large financial institution that was having difficulty implementing a new marketing program. The president of the company defined the problem this way: "We're trying to get our people in our branch offices to be more assertive in offering our products and services. Rather than just passively attending to our customers' current needs, we'd like our employees to actively assess the future needs of our clients and recommend products that would meet those needs. Unfortunately, we've not seen much success since we rolled out this new program six months ago." He then asked: "Can you help us find out what's wrong and what to do about it?"

We agreed to help him, and decided that our first order of business would be to interview the branch managers as well as a select number of branch employees throughout the company. As we conducted the interviews, we asked why they were having such difficulty implementing the program. Some of the more common answers were: "I think we're here to provide service—not to be salesmen"; "I don't really understand how the program works—more training would be helpful"; and "I'm not sure there are enough incentives to get us to do this new program."

After hearing these reports, we then asked the branch managers what they were doing to help their employees work through these issues. We often heard answers like this: "We'd like to work through these issues with our team of employees in our branch, but we don't have time to work with them and deal with the problems we face. The branch opens at 9 a.m. and we arrive about 8:30 a.m. to get prepared for the day. Then the branch closes at 5 p.m. and we take about a half hour to finish up and leave. We're only paid from 8:30 a.m. until 5:30 p.m., and we don't want to spend time off the clock to work on these issues. However, if we were paid to spend an hour or so a week to solve problems in the branch—maybe we could meet early in the morning or after work one day a week—then I think we could get something done. Having a branch team meeting once a week is a good idea, but the president wouldn't pay us to do it. He's a bit of a miser."

Armed with this information, we met with the president and gave him this feedback. He asked: "Do you think we'll see improvement if we pay our employees to meet once a week for an hour?" We told him, "You likely won't see any improvement in the implementation of this program unless your branch teams are incentivized to meet each week and address the problems they face implementing the program." The president agreed to start paying his employees to spend time at team meetings each week addressing not only the implementation of this program, but other problems they were experiencing.

Most teams decided to meet before work started on Monday morning. Not surprisingly, performance in the branches began to improve, and the new marketing initiative began to be implemented more effectively. Moreover, based on feedback from employees generated during these meetings the president also decided that he need to launch a more aggressive television advertising campaign to further support the marketing efforts of his employees in the branches. In short, the branch teams, now rewarded for having team meetings, and receiving more support from the corporate office, were much more effective than they had been in the past.

The Importance of Context

What we have learned from our own experience in consulting with teams over the years is this: context matters! Without a team-supportive organizational context, creating effective teams is difficult, even impossible. The president of the financial institution couldn't get the teams in his branches to even meet together for any length of time because the context didn't support teamwork—there were no incentives for the teams to meet on a regular basis. To create an organizational context that will support teamwork, the team needs to consider a variety of factors which we will address in this chapter.

How Important Is Teamwork for the Team to Succeed?

Although all teams represent a collection of people who must collaborate to some degree to achieve common goals, some tasks require more collaboration than others. Figure 2.1 represents a continuum of the teamwork or collaboration needed for a team to function. The continuum is based on the notion that the importance of teamwork will vary according to the task environment, notably the degree of interdependence required to complete the team's tasks.

Modular Interdependence Sometimes the nature of the task doesn't require the team to work closely together because the team tasks are largely individual in nature. With these types of tasks, individuals on the team are connected through what is called *modular* or *pooled interdependence*, performing tasks independently and pooling only the results to create a team output. For example, a golf team may do some general planning and share information about the golf course, give each other tips on how to hit certain

Figure 2.1 Continuum of Teamwork

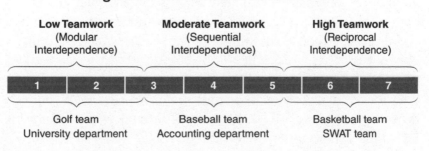

shots, or give each other information about the competition, but in the final analysis, play is by the individual performer. Likewise, some sales teams are comprised of team members who work individually and only meet periodically to share ideas or get feedback on their performance. Team performance is based on individual performances that are pooled together.

Similarly, an academic department requires relatively little teamwork. Each professor can do most of the required work—teach, research, write—alone. Of course, faculty members share ideas on how to be effective in teaching and research. But the performance of the department, as measured by student teaching evaluations or the number of faculty publications in top journals, is based largely on individual performances that are pooled together. When important decisions need to be made or departmental goals set that require the efforts of all department members, then those members must function as a decision-making team. However, these situations occur relatively infrequently.

Sequential Interdependence Individuals on teams are *sequentially interdependent* when one person cannot perform his or her task until another has completed his or her task and passed on the results. Under these circumstances, team members must meet more regularly and consistently to coordinate their work.

A baseball team is an example of a team that requires a moderate amount of teamwork. All nine players must be on the field at once, but for much of the game, the effort is individual in nature. However, whether a batter bunts or tries to hit to the opposite field depends on what the previous hitters have done. Relay throws from outfield to home base and double plays require sequential coordination. Moreover, the catcher and pitcher interact constantly in a coordinated fashion as they try to prevent batters from reaching the home plate.

An accounting or financial department requires sequential coordination. Everyone in the department must work within a common accounting framework, and the work of one part of the accounting financial process depends on the work of other parts. The accuracy of the tax people depends in part on how well internal auditors have done their work in accurately identifying relevant firm revenues and expenses. Although each accountant may be doing individual work, each sometimes may be unable to proceed without input from others.

Most company executive committees require a moderate amount of teamwork. Historically, for much of their work, the heads of marketing, finance, personnel, and manufacturing have done their work autonomously in their own areas. At key times, they come together to build a common strategy, set common goals, and coordinate work activities, such as getting marketing and manufacturing to agree on the type and amount of product that should be produced for the marketplace. However, effective companies now realize that success in coordinating product development and manufacturing, or manufacturing and sales and marketing activities, requires what we call "reciprocal" rather than sequential interdependence.

Reciprocal Interdependence In some groups, the nature of the task requires a high degree of teamwork because tasks are *reciprocally interdependent*. Team results are achieved through work done in a simultaneous and iterative process in which each individual must work in close coordination with other team members because he or she can complete tasks only through a process of iterative knowledge sharing and the coordination of one another's efforts. Team members must communicate their own requirements frequently and be responsive to the needs of the other team members. They must adjust in real time to meet the needs of other members of the team.

Similarly, members of a basketball team are on the court together and must coordinate constantly as they run offense plays and play team defense. Every member interacts with every other member. Thus, one would predict that a basketball team would suffer more from the lack of teamwork than would a golf team or even a baseball team. Indeed, this seems to be the case, as evidenced by the fact that major league baseball teams that acquire a few free agent stars occasionally come from a low-ranking team the prior year (even last place) to win the World Series. This happens less often with basketball teams, which must learn how to coordinate and work together to be successful.

Product development teams for complex products such as automobiles, aircraft, robotics, and consumer electronics work together in a reciprocally interdependent fashion. For example, when a commercial aircraft is being designed, decisions regarding the weight and thrust of a jet engine as well as the aerodynamic design of the fuselage and wings must be made taking each other into account. Team members must share information back and forth as they iteratively solve problems. Similar arguments could be made for a police SWAT team or the surgical team in a hospital operating room. All of these tasks are highly connected, and members cannot do their respective work without others doing theirs in a coordinated fashion.

Understanding the level of teamwork and the nature of interdependence required by the task is important for three reasons. First, they dictate the amount of attention that managers need to pay to teamwork and team processes: the greater the team interdependence, the more important it is to make sure the team is working together effectively, and that everyone understands the nature of the interdependence. Second, by understanding the nature of interdependencies in the team, managers will have greater insight into why certain common problems arise and will know how to fix them. For example, team members of modularly interdependent tasks frequently feel frustrated when team processes are designed for frequent meetings and interaction. They rightly want to be left alone to get their work done rather than be bothered by group processes. Similarly, highly interdependent teams often run into trouble when they have few opportunities for frequent, rich interactions. Third, understanding the different levels of teamwork and the nature of interdependence will allow managers to adapt business and team structures to the nature of the task and thereby prevent some problems from occurring in the first place.

The Role of Top Management

Senior managers in an organization generally set the tone for the use of teams in the organization. We find that in some organizations, senior managers prefer not to use teams and teamwork extensively, preferring to make decisions by themselves or in one-on-one conversations with other key managers. Also, senior managers often don't know how to run effective team meetings so they are poor role models for their subordinates. We've been to many senior management meetings that unfortunately were poorly organized, with unclear objectives, and many on the team not focused on the agenda item at hand, preferring to have quiet side conversations with one another. Effective teamwork starts at the top!

Some senior managers encourage teamwork by recognizing the importance of teamwork in the organization's mission or values statement. For example, Bain & Company, one of the world's most successful management consulting firms, has in their mission statement that Bain & Company is a *community of extraordinary teams*. Indeed, since Bain's clients are served by consulting teams, they must be excellent for the company as a whole to succeed. *Extraordinary teams* is a term that you hear often within Bain & Company. They create these teams by placing a senior director responsible for researching and understanding what makes an extraordinary team at Bain. This senior executive then gives a report at the annual company meeting on the company's progress in this area. An extraordinary team is selected and featured in the biannual company newsletter with a description of how and why the team is extraordinary. These teams were also recognized at the company meetings and celebrated with a team "event." All teams within the company are encouraged—and given the resources—to celebrate successful projects or particularly effective teamwork. Celebrating can range from a team dinner to a weekend of skiing together. Senior managers want to let the team know that they appreciate a job well done. When top management devotes its own resources to developing and recognizing teamwork, they create a context within which teamwork can thrive.

Reward Systems

Rewards for team performance are also very powerful in encouraging teamwork. Bain & Company employees are given both time and incentives for them to function effectively as a team. Most organizations focus their reward systems on individual achievement—your bonus or your annual raise is predicated on how well you performed individually. Such an approach makes sense when only pooled interdependence is needed and therefore individual contributions are the key to success.

However, in many cases, sequential or reciprocal interdependence is required to get work accomplished, and therefore team members must cooperate and coordinate their efforts to achieve the team's goals. Progressive organizations recognize this and have as part of their performance evaluations (1) the individual team member's contribution to team performance, and (2) the overall performance of the team. Thus, team members are not fully rewarded if only they, and not their team, succeed. Furthermore, coordination between various teams in the organization is often needed for the organization to achieve its goals as well. Hence, some type of reward system, such as profit sharing that rewards individuals if the entire organization is successful, encourages cooperation between various departments and teams within the organization.

Amazon is a company that works hard to get employees to feel like owners and builders of the entire company, not just individual business units. "Our performance appraisal and compensation scheme rewards ownership," Jeff Wilke, CEO of Amazon's retail operations, told us. "It rewards doing the right thing for the whole company, not optimizing your part of the company."[1]

We find that successful organizations today use multiple criteria—individual, team, and organizational—to determine pay raises and bonuses. For example, an organization might base its bonuses using the following percentages: 40 percent on individual achievement, 40 percent on team achievement, and 20 percent on the achievement of organizational goals. Thus, someone would receive 100 percent of his or her bonus if the goals were achieved in all three areas. The bonus would decrease by the corresponding percentage if performance was unsatisfactory in one or more of the areas. In this way, organizations can focus an employee's attention not only on individual achievement but also on achieving the goals of the team and organization.

Feedback Systems

Teams need good information to function effectively. Without such feedback it's difficult, if not impossible, for the team to improve and make course corrections. If you wanted to sail a boat from Los Angeles, California, to Hawaii, you would not simply point your boat at Hawaii and take off without ever again checking your bearings. Wind, waves, and tides would all pull your boat in different directions. Without frequently and consistently receiving feedback about your path through GPS and other navigational tools, and making constant course corrections, you would never reach your destination.

Leading a team to a desired destination is the same. You can't just set it up and assume it will function perfectly without continual feedback regarding how it is performing. Bain & Company is a good example of a company that provides effective feedback to its teams through its information systems. Overall team satisfaction and team leadership effectiveness are evaluated every month through a formal review process. Members fill out a survey and rate their satisfaction on such issues as:

- Value addition and impact of work
- Ability of team leaders to motivate and inspire team members
- Clear and prompt downward communication
- Reasonable time demands
- Up-front planning and organization
- Fun, motivation, and a sense of teamwork
- Interest level of work
- Clear performance expectations

- Level of responsibility
- Opportunities for professional growth and development
- General level of respect for each person

The data are compiled and given to both the team members and the team's leaders (manager and partner). The team then meets alone, without the team leaders, to discuss the results and to develop recommendations regarding what could be done to improve team satisfaction and performance. Likewise, team leaders meet to develop their own recommendations. Then the team members and leaders meet together to discuss each other's recommendations to determine what should be done to improve team satisfaction and performance over the next month. In cases where the team satisfaction scores are particularly low, a facilitator will meet with the entire team to facilitate a team-building discussion.

Team satisfaction and performance scores are posted publicly each month so team leaders have strong incentives to ensure that they are taking actions that improve team satisfaction if scores are low. When asked whether monthly reviews were too frequent, Krista Ridgeway, a partner in the Chicago office, said, "We used to do reviews every two months in the Chicago office and thought that was enough. But the other offices started doing it every month and we eventually decided we would give it a try. We discovered that we were able to discover and respond to team problems much more quickly when we did it monthly. Problems were less likely to escalate. And it really only takes people about 5 minutes to do the evaluation, so we've found that it is definitely worth the effort." Bain teams also get regular performance data on how their clients are performing related to the goals the client wants to achieve—a key measure of team success. Armed with these data, Bain team members know how their team is performing in relationship to other teams within Bain as well as how their client is performing. There is no question that developing processes and systems that provide accurate and timely data to teams regarding team functioning and performance is part of a context that allows teams to thrive.

Organization Structure and Team Performance

Structure refers to the basic design of the organization as represented in an organization chart. It reflects authority, communication patterns, and the responsibility for certain functions in the organization. Organization structure largely determines who works with whom and whether teams are designated formally to carry out organization tasks. Although all organizations have informal groups that form for a variety of reasons, the formal organization structure can encourage and support teamwork, or it can make it much more difficult for teams to form and function effectively. The structure also typically determines the authority a team has to make decisions and implement them. For a team to be effective, the proper authority needs to be delegated to the team through the organization's structure. Furthermore, the role of the team within the organization can have a significant impact on team members. If team members feel that the role of the team is important to the organization, then they will likely feel more committed to the team and to helping it achieve its goals.

We have also found that organizations which rely on a structure which fails to account for the teamwork that occurs across the various functions (engineering, marketing, manufacturing, and so on) tend to foster conflict, miscommunication, and poor coordination. To illustrate, Chrysler experienced teamwork problems in developing new cars up through the early 1990s when it was organized around functional silos in engineering, manufacturing, finance, marketing, and purchasing. New cars were developed in temporary project teams that pulled individuals from each of the functional areas. However, using this organizational structure, Chrysler took six years to develop a new car, while its Japanese competitors, Toyota and Honda, were consistently developing new cars in four years. Chrysler realized that its organizational structure was one of the problems.

To address the teamwork problem, Chrysler reorganized around car platform teams: large car, small car, truck, and minivan. In this way, individuals from the different functional areas worked together consistently within the same team over long periods of time. This structure even brought supplier partners onto the team—giving the supplier "guest engineers" desks and workspace within the platform team.

This reorganization improved teamwork and coordination within the product development teams at Chrysler. Within three years, they were developing new car models on a four-year basis, just like their Japanese competitors. Chrysler's experience shows that organizations that are designed based on a team concept can use organization structure to bring people together in formal, and sometimes informal, teams to accomplish the organization's goals.

Organizational Culture and Teamwork

An organization's culture is a context variable that plays a powerful role in team development. An organization's culture represents the basic shared values and assumptions held by most people in the organization. It defines what things are viewed as right or wrong, what is valued, how one gets into trouble, and how people are expected to see the world around them. It is critical to a teamwork-focused organization that the shared cultural rules emphasize that teamwork is essential to advance one's career and that people at all levels get into trouble if they do not collaborate with others and respond readily to the needs of their team. If the culture is either openly or passively resistant to the importance of teamwork, any attempts to foster collaboration, participation, or involvement will be seen as a temporary action or management manipulation.

In one organization we studied, the culture was permeated by one key assumption or basic rule: no one does anything without checking with Fred, the CEO, first. The rule was clearly demonstrated each time an employee walked past the thermostat in the hall and read the sign: DO NOT ADJUST THIS THERMOSTAT WITHOUT FRED'S PERMISSION!!! In an atmosphere in which one must wait for the boss before taking any action, it is difficult to encourage teamwork and collaboration. It is important for team members to clearly understand which types of decisions and actions require a leader's approval and which ones the team members are empowered to make.

For example, at Amazon leaders teach employees to distinguish between "one-way door" (costly to reverse) decisions and "two-way door" (reversible at low cost) decisions. "We want to have a start-up culture and start-up companies make decisions very quickly," Jeff Bezos, CEO of Amazon, told us.

> "In larger companies there are certain decisions that are so momentous and so hard to reverse that appropriately you should use a very deliberate decision-making process that takes time. Those are 'one-way door' decisions. One of the things that slows large companies down is that all decisions end up being made with that heavy weighted process; even ones that are reversible. To prevent that we constantly teach the difference and when you see examples of something reversible being made with a heavy-weight decision-making process you need to highlight it and say: 'Why is this happening, what's going on?' Our goal is to have the scale and scope of a large company but the heart and spirit of a small one."[2]

Developing a culture that creates a supportive context for teamwork—such as speed of decision making—is important to helping teams work productively.

Physical Space and Teamwork

The last context factor that we will consider is that of physical space. We know from both research and experience that people interact with one another more frequently if they are located close to each other. Thus, having team members co-located by one another is a significant advantage for the team, especially if the team's tasks require reciprocal interdependence. Teams also need to have space to meet and do their work together. So, whether it be a large conference room or some other facility, it must be readily accessible to the team. Finally, team members may also need to meet privately with one another to discuss confidential matters. This is particularly true for the team leader who may want to have a confidential conversation with a team member or when team members have a disagreement with one another and they may want to discuss their differences in private. Thus, the arrangement of the team's physical space can either help or hinder teamwork.

Assessing Whether the Organization's Context Supports Teamwork

In this chapter we have argued that one reason for poor team performance is the lack of congruence between an organization's context and teamwork. To avoid this problem, an organization should periodically assess how these context factors—the need for teamwork, top management support, reward systems, feedback systems, structure, culture, and physical space—are affecting teamwork in the organization. The following assessment could be used for this purpose. After such an assessment, management can take corrective action to ensure that the organization's context supports teamwork.

Team Context Scale

Instructions: Using your observations of your organization and work unit or team, circle the number that applies to each question (on a scale of 1 to 5).

1. Is teamwork needed for your team to accomplish its goals (e.g. are team members highly interdependent?)

1	2	3	4	5
No, not really.		It is somewhat important.		Teamwork is critical to success.

---

2. Do the organization's senior managers encourage teamwork?

1	2	3	4	5
No, teamwork is not encouraged.		Teamwork is somewhat encouraged.		Teamwork is encouraged by senior management.

3. Does the organization's reward system encourage teamwork?

1	2	3	4	5
No, teamwork is not encouraged.		Teamwork is somewhat encouraged.		Teamwork is encouraged as part of the organization's reward system.

4. Does the organization encourage teamwork across team (e.g. department, functional unit) boundaries?

1	2	3	4	5
No, teamwork is not encouraged across team boundaries.		Teamwork is somewhat encouraged across team boundaries.		Teamwork is encouraged across team boundaries.

(Continued)

5. Does the organization have information systems that provide useful data on team functioning and performance?

1	2	3	4	5
No, the information systems hinder teamwork.		The information systems somewhat support teamwork.		Yes, the information systems support teamwork.

6. Is the team's role in the organization clear in how it contributes to the organization's goals?

1	2	3	4	5
No, the role is unclear.		The role is somewhat clear.		Yes, the role is very clear.

7. Does the organization's structure (organization chart, roles, job descriptions, and so on) support teamwork?

1	2	3	4	5
No, the structure hinders teamwork.		The structure somewhat supports teamwork.		Yes, the structure supports teamwork.

8. Does the team have the authority within the organizational structure that is needed to accomplish its goals?

1	2	3	4	5
No, the team has little authority.		It has some authority, but not all that is needed.		Yes, the team has the authority it needs.

9. Does the organization's culture (its rules and values) encourage teamwork?

1	2	3	4	5
No, teamwork is not encouraged.		Teamwork is somewhat encouraged.		Teamwork is encouraged as part of the organization's culture.

10. Does the organization's physical space encourage teamwork?

1	2	3	4	5
No, teamwork is not encouraged by the physical space.		Teamwork is somewhat encouraged.		Teamwork is encouraged as part of the organization's physical space.

(Continued)

Scoring: Add up your score and divide by 10.

A score of 3.75 or higher indicates that the organization's context generally supports team performance.

Scores between 2.5 and 3.75 indicate moderate support for team performance.

Scores between 1.0 and 2.5 indicate some serious problems related to context that are hindering team performance.

If responses to even one or two items are very low (1 or 2), this suggests that action may need to be taken soon to improve the context. However, if the response to item 1 (the need for teamwork) is low (either a 1 or 2), which typically means that the interdependence of team members is largely pooled or sequential, then the mean score may not need to be as high as in a team in which teamwork is essential to achieve its goals (in other words, when there is a need for reciprocal interdependence).

Notes

1. Personal interview, July 31, 2018.
2. Personal interview, July 31, 2018.

3

COMPOSITION: PUTTING THE RIGHT PEOPLE ON THE TEAM

If the organization's context is supportive of teamwork, the next task is to determine the size of the team, who should be on the team, and how team members should be managed depending on their skillset and motivation. In this chapter, we will explore these issues and provide an assessment instrument for evaluating the composition of a team.

Team Composition and Performance

For a team to succeed, its members need two things: 1) the skills to accomplish goals laid out for the team, and 2) "fire in the belly," that is, the motivation to succeed. In addition, research has shown that successful teams are comprised of team members who also have the following characteristics:[1]

- Effective interpersonal and communication skills
- A willingness to help and support other team members in their efforts to achieve team goals
- Good conflict management skills
- Ability to adapt to new situations
- Dependability and ability to take initiative to help the team achieve its goals

Effective team leaders understand that the way they manage the team and individual team members is strongly influenced by the

35

Figure 3.1 Team Composition: Evaluating and Managing Team Members Based on Skills and Motivation

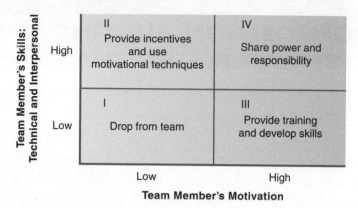

degree to which team members are both skilled and motivated (see Figure 3.1). In some instances, team members may not have the necessary background and skills, or may not be properly motivated to work on the team, as seen in quadrant I of Figure 3.1. When team members are neither skilled nor motivated, team leaders may be wise to drop them from the team because the challenge of building their skills and motivating them is simply too daunting.

When team members are skilled but not motivated (quadrant II), the team leader's role is largely a motivational one. We have found that empowering skilled team members with greater responsibility for team tasks and performance can be an effective way to increase a team member's commitment to the team and its goals. Naturally, it is preferable if team members are intrinsically rather than extrinsically motivated. In fact, when selecting someone for the team, it is important to determine to what extent the person has a passion and love for this kind of work, and to what extent she or he is committed to the team goals.

In contrast, when team members are in quadrant III, that is, motivated but not skilled, the leader's task is largely one of coaching and skill building. This requires that the leader play the roles of educator and coach. It also means that assessments of skill deficiencies are necessary so that an individual development and training program can be established to ensure that the person develops the skills necessary to be effective in completing the team's tasks.

The ideal team members are those from quadrant IV. These team members are both skilled and motivated. In this case, the wise team leader will share power and responsibility with team members, since they are capable of assisting the leader in developing team competencies and are motivated to achieve the team's goals.

As teams are formed, team leaders should meet with potential team members before selection to ascertain their ability to contribute to the accomplishment of the team's goals as well as their motivation to be part of the team. Offering a meaningful team goal or significant performance challenge generally can rally individuals to a team and motivate them. When team members believe they are being asked to contribute to something important—something that counts, that has vision—they are more likely to give their best effort than will people who are asked to serve on another team or committee that seems to serve little purpose (see sidebar: Setting a Lofty Vision to Attract Talent to Your Team).

Setting a Lofty Vision to Attract Talent to Your Team

Our examination of the world's most innovative leaders revealed an interesting leadership pattern that is used by many successful leaders. In the book *Innovation Capital* we call it the "Virtuous Innovation Leadership Cycle." The cycle begins by identifying a lofty vision for creating value that attracts others to your team.

Whatever your view of Elon Musk, one thing Musk did when he helped launch Tesla was articulate a lofty vision for the company. "Our goal is to accelerate the advent of sustainable transport by bringing compelling mass market electric cars to market as soon as possible," he wrote. "In order to get to that goal, big leaps in technology are required." Musk then laid out his "master plan"—a strategy for launching desirable electric vehicles at the high end of the market followed by affordable electric vehicles for the mainstream market.

(Continued)

When launching SpaceX Musk announced that the company goal was "to revolutionize space technology with the ultimate goal of enabling people to live on other planets." When Tesla pursued the Powerwall—a product that uses batteries to power homes and utilities (and, of course, charge your Tesla vehicle)—Musk announced that "we are trying to change the fundamental energy structure of the world." He even makes the creation of a big battery sound exciting!

Sterling Anderson, former head of Tesla Model X, Tesla AutoPilot and co-founder of Aurora Innovation (a start-up that provides a full stack self-driving solution for major automakers like Volkswagen and Hyundai), believes that Musk's success as an innovative leader stems largely from a reinforcing cycle of success that is triggered by an exciting and inspirational vision. Says Anderson:

> Elon understands people. He understands that a lofty vision, an inspirational vision, attracts world class people, particularly world class engineers. With those world class engineers he's able to build a better product. That better product attracts customers and attracts investors, and it's self-reinforcing. As this feeds on itself, engineers are increasingly inspired to join, not only because of the lofty vision but also because of the increasingly strong brand behind it. These conditions attract increasingly strong talent; it feels good to work there and to be viewed as someone who is helping drive innovation towards that lofty goal.

Musk understands that painting an exciting and important vision can be an important tool for getting talented people on his team. But it doesn't have to be something as lofty as reducing global warming or putting a colony on Mars. PepsiCo CEO Indra Nooyi was able to do this with PepsiCo's beverage and snack foods business by introducing "Performance with Purpose," a mission to make the world a better place by focusing on making healthier products and by creating a sustainable food system. Says Nooyi: "Performance with purpose is about how we as a company replenish the planet and leave the world a better place."

Amazon.com is known for attracting and retaining some of the best and brightest technical talent around. It does this in part by maintaining one constant in its selection process: "Does this candidate have a strong desire to change the world?" Leaders are looking for people who want to achieve something important. In addition, job applicants are interviewed by teams of Amazon employees—in many cases, by the entire team that they will join. Team interviews often focus on finding new members who will bring diversity to the team (which is critical for innovation and is an explicit goal of the team interviews) and tests whether the recruits have the collaboration skills necessary to succeed in Amazon's team environment.

Team Size

There is no clear answer as to the size of an optimal team because size is determined in part by the nature of the task. Some managers like large teams because they believe that these teams generate more ideas and call attention to the importance of a project or functional area. Moreover, some managers think that putting people on a team is a good experience, and they don't want to leave anyone out. However, in general, small teams are preferable to large teams, and there are rules of thumb and certain pitfalls to avoid in determining team size.[2]

We find that large teams (typically over ten people) have lower productivity than smaller teams. Research reported by Katzenbach and Smith in their book *The Wisdom of Teams* suggests that "serious deterioration in the quality and productivity of team interactions sets in when there are more than 12 to 14 members of the team."[2] The greater the number of team members, the more difficult it is to achieve a common understanding and agreement about team goals and team processes. Large teams lead to less involvement on the part of team members and hence lower commitment and participation, which leads to lower levels of trust.

Although team size clearly should be determined by the nature of the task, much of the research suggests that the most productive teams have four to ten members. In summarizing research on team size, researcher Glenn Parker notes, "Although optimal size depends on the specific team mission, in general, the optimal team size is four to six members, with ten being the maximum for effectiveness. It is important to remember that many team tools in decision making, problem solving, and communicating were created to take advantage of small-group dynamics. Consensus, for example, just does not work as a decision-making method in a team of twenty members."[3]

Amazon.com has experienced an explosion of growth throughout its short life and employs thousands of people. However, whenever possible, it deploys its workforce into "two-pizza" teams (the number of people who can be adequately fed by two pizzas) to promote team identity and foster commitment, accountability, and innovation within the team. Because two large pizzas typically feed six to ten people, you rarely find larger teams within Amazon. Thus, the rule of thumb is to choose the smallest number of people possible that will still allow the team to effectively accomplish its mission.

Personality Tests in Selecting Team Members

A number of companies today use personality tests as part of the selection process for employment and for assignment to teams. Personality tests that are often used include the Myers-Briggs Type Indicator (MBTI) and the Personality Characteristics Inventory (PCI), but there are literally hundreds of such tests out on the market today.

Unfortunately, most of the research on the relationship between personality and job performance shows a very weak correlation. One study that reviewed the academic literature on the subject noted that correlations between personality and job performance typically fell in the .03 to .15 range—meaning that about 90 percent of the variance in job performance was *not* explained by personality factors.[4] Context variables, the nature of the task, the individual's job skills and knowledge, and so on play a much larger role in a team member's performance.

While personality tests might prove to be useful with some teams in certain situations—tests deemed to be reliable and valid—we suggest that such tests be used as only a part of the picture when determining team composition. Team leaders should primarily look at the team members' skills, prior work experience, interest and motivation to work on the team, ability to work well with others, and so on as the criteria to be used when creating a team or adding new members to the team.

The Problem Team Member

One question we're often asked is: What do you do when one member of the team continually blocks the progress of the rest of the team? This person may always take a contrary point of view, vote against proposals everyone else supports, take a negative or pessimistic position on everything, and frequently miss meetings or not follow through on assignments.

The obvious question in response is: Why do you keep a person like that on the team? As we suggested earlier, team members without the requisite skills and motivation should be dropped from the team. However, sometimes the person has some needed competencies, or is a long-term employee, and terminating or transferring him or her can create additional problems as well. If a manager or supervisor is trying to build a team and one person won't buy into the process, some method of removing that person from the team or changing his or her assignment should be considered. Many executives, after feeling the need to cut someone from the team, express the sentiment that they wished they had done it sooner—or at least would have provided feedback and corrective action sooner.

The following kinds of actions have also been found to be successful in some (not all) cases.

1. *Direct confrontation between the team leader and the problem person.* This may give the supervisor an opportunity to describe clearly the problem behaviors and the consequences if such behaviors do not change.

2. *Confrontation by the group.* If only the team leader deals with the problem person, the conflict may be perceived by that person as just the personal bias of the leader. In a case like this, it would be better for the group to deal directly with the problem member collectively in a team meeting. The team members' feedback to the problem team member must be descriptive, not evaluative. They must describe the problem behavior and identify the negative consequences of the behaviors—all without punitive, negative evaluations of the individual personally.

3. *Special responsibility.* It has been found for some difficult people that giving them a more important role in the team increases their commitment to the team process. The person might be asked to be the team recorder, the agenda builder, or the one to summarize the discussion of issues. One team even rotated the difficult member into the role of *acting* team leader with the responsibility for a limited time of getting team agreement on the issues at hand.

4. *Limited participation.* One team asked the problem person to attend meetings, listen but not participate in the team activities, and then have a one-to-one session with the team leader. If the leader felt that the member had some legitimate issues to raise, the leader would present them to the group at the next meeting, but in all cases the decision of the team would be final.

5. *External assignment.* At times it may be possible to give the problem person an assignment outside the activities of the rest of the team. The person may make a contribution to the work unit on an individual basis, whereas the bulk of the work that requires collaboration is handled by the rest of the team.

All of these suggestions can be useful when a person is a serious obstruction to the team. One must always be careful, however, to differentiate the real problem person from someone who sees things differently and whose different views or perspectives need to be listened to and considered with the possibility that this may enrich the productivity of the team. Teams can get *too* cohesive and isolate a person who is different.

Getting the Right People on the Team: How Bain & Company Does It

Getting the right people on the team is a critical step for Bain & Company as it focuses its recruiting efforts at top universities around the globe. Bain, which was named the number-one company in the United States to work for in 2019 by Glassdoor, identifies these universities as being able to effectively find (and sometimes prepare) individuals for management consulting. Bain also invests heavily in multiple rounds of interviews with new recruits as it looks for three skill sets: analytical and problem-solving skills, communication and client management skills, and team collaboration skills.

In the first round of interviews, recruits are largely tested on their analytical and problem-solving skills as they are asked to solve business cases during the interviews. The second round focuses more on whether recruits have the client and communication skills necessary and whether they will be effective team players. As part of the client and communication skill evaluation, interviewers assess whether the person has the appropriate degree of confidence and optimism without showing arrogance. They also assess whether a recruit can comfortably communicate with all sorts of people, from shop foreman to CEO. Finally, recruits must pass the airplane test: "Is this someone I would want to hang out with for six hours on an airplane?" "Is this someone I want to work on *my* team?"

Another way that Bain gets the right people is to watch them perform on a Bain team before they are hired as a full-time consultant. To do this, Bain invests heavily in a summer intern program, bringing in a large number of MBA and undergraduate students to work over the summer to see whether they have the right stuff (i.e. analytical skills, communication skills, and team collaboration skills). Thus, Bain puts potential team members on a simulated "bus ride" before putting them on the bus for good.

According to Mark Howorth, senior director of global recruiting for Bain, roughly two-thirds of new consultants hired have worked at Bain either as summer interns or as analysts (associate consultants) after graduating from college. This dramatically reduces the risk of getting the wrong people on the bus. Once Bain has determined that a person has the ability to be successful, it brings that person into an organizational environment that supports effective teamwork.

Bain's internal study of extraordinary teams found that lower-performing teams were generally larger and had multiple reporting relationships. Consequently, efforts are made to keep teams small and structures flat. The logic is that people work harder and are happier when they are given heavy responsibility and are not burdened by layers of management. Moreover, on a small team, individuals have more direction from supervisors and are less likely to get lost in the shuffle and end up frustrated and unproductive. Therefore, teams are generally organized to consist of only four to six members. These individuals report to a manager, who then reports to a partner, the end of the line of authority. All are closely involved in the work and are held accountable for team performance.

Bain devotes significant time to determining the right mix of people given the demands of the team project and the professional development needs of potential team members. The team assignment process begins with a discussion among the office staffing officer, partners or managers, and potential members. The staffing officer typically discusses the skills required to be successful on a particular client project with the partner or manager. Three issues are generally reviewed when a person is considered for a team:

1. Does this person have the skills and experience necessary to help the client be successful in this particular assignment?
2. Does this project fit with this person's skill plan and professional development needs?
3. Will this person work well with the client, manager, and other team members?

The staffing officer in charge of case team assignments speaks with managers and potential team members before an assignment is made to make sure the fit is good. In most cases potential team members can refuse an assignment if they make a strong argument that they cannot answer these questions with a "yes." By taking time in advance to consider these issues, Bain ensures that team members are considerably more committed to the team and are less likely to become frustrated and unproductive. As a result, management saves time by avoiding team problems down the road.

This may seem paradoxical, but while creating extraordinary teams is the overall goal, Bain doesn't lose sight of the fact that extraordinary teams are composed of successful and productive individuals. To ensure that individual needs are considered, professional development is a company priority. Managers and team members jointly develop skill plans to outline the skills that the team member needs to develop in order to advance in the organization.

Skill plans are prepared every six months with the manager providing coaching and feedback. Most managers also conduct a monthly or bimonthly lunch with each member to discuss professional development needs. The system is supported by a professional development department whose primary responsibility is to help employees with their personal growth and development. Team "buddies," or colleagues, are assigned when a new member joins the company to ensure that he or she is properly integrated into the team. Remembering the individual is Bain's way of keeping its turnover among the lowest in the consulting industry.

Creating a New Team: The Case of the Smith Family Business

Several years ago, we were approach by Barbara Smith (family names changed to protect their identities) to help her with her family-owned business. She had created a very successful retail

(*Continued*)

operation that she managed with her two sons and her daughter. She was nearing retirement and wanted to develop a plan to turn over the ownership and management of the business to her three children. But she had some questions:

- Are my children prepared to take over the family business?
- How do I transfer ownership to my children? Should I give them the stock or should I sell it to them?
- What role should I play in the future after I retire?
- How do I provide help and support for my children as they move into their new roles as owners and managers?
- What can we do to help our business grow?

To help Barbara answer these questions we suggested that she create a new team—a board of advisors—that could help her work through these issues. As we thought about these issues it was clear that she needed a board with expertise on the following: (1) how to manage succession in a family business; (2) how to manage the transfer of stock as well as a variety of other financial transactions; and (3) how to help the business compete more successfully in the marketplace.

Given these needs, Barbara had Gibb (an expert at family business succession), Tom (the firm's accountant and financial advisor), and Fred (a well-known entrepreneur and expert on the industry) appointed to the board of advisors. Barbara and her two sons represented the family on the board. The board met each quarter and focused on the issues listed previously.

Furthermore, the outside board members were also charged with evaluating the performance of the family members in the business, giving the family members some outside, objective feedback on how they were doing and providing them with some suggestions and guidance on how to improve. Over a period of a few years, the board helped the family accomplish the following:

- Transfer ownership and management to the next generation.
- Move Barbara into a consulting role which allowed her to continue to help the business even though she was no longer an

owner. It also allowed her to get some additional income for her work.

- Broaden the strategic focus of the business to help it move into new markets.
- Manage several family interpersonal issues and dynamics that could have stymied the transfer of ownership.
- Develop plans for personal improvement on the part of Barbara's children.

As a result of these changes, the business' revenues have doubled in size and family members have generally worked well together—something that is often not the case in family-owned firms. Thus, creating a new team—a board of advisors with the right people on it—provided the support the family needed to help it manage the succession process and help the business grow.

Assessing Composition

Because composition is important for team success, we believe that organizations should periodically do an assessment to see if their methods for assigning team members support team development. The following worksheet provides an assessment for determining whether that foundation is in place.

Team Composition Scale

Instructions: Using your observations of your organization and work unit or team, circle the number that applies to each question (on a scale of 1 to 5).

1. Does your organization have a well-thought-out method for assigning people to be on a team?

(Continued)

1	2	3	4	5
No, team assignments are rather haphazard.		Some thought goes into team assignments.		Yes, careful thought is taken before making team assignments.

2. Is your team comprised of team members with the necessary technical skills, knowledge and experience to achieve its goals?

1	2	3	4	5
No, it needs more skills, knowledge, and experience.		It has some of the skills, knowledge, and experience it needs.		Yes, it has all the skills, knowledge, and experience it needs.

3. Do team members have the interpersonal skills needed to work effectively as a team?

1	2	3	4	5
No, they don't have the interpersonal skills needed.		They have some of the interpersonal skills needed.		Yes, they have the interpersonal skills needed to work well as a team.

4. Is the team the appropriate size to accomplish its goals?

1	2	3	4	5
No, it is either too large or too small.		The team might need to add or subtract a member or two.		Yes, the team is the right size for the task.

5. Are team members motivated to help the team achieve its goals?

1	2	3	4	5
No, there is little motiva- tion.		There is some motivation on the part of team members.		Yes, team members are highly motivated to achieve team goals.

Scoring: Add up your score and divide by 5.

A score of 3.75 or higher indicates that the team's composition generally supports team performance.

Scores between 2.5 and 3.75 indicate moderate support for team performance.

Scores between 1.0 and 2.5 indicate some serious problems related to composition that are hindering team performance.

If responses to even one or two items are very low (1 or 2), this suggests that action may need to be taken soon to improve the team's composition.

Notes

1. L. C. McDermott, N. Brawley, and W. W. Waite, *World Class Teams: Working Across Borders* (New York: Wiley, 1998).
2. J. R. Katzenbach and D. K. Smith, *The Wisdom of Teams* (New York: HarperCollins, 2003), 275.
3. G. M. Parker, *Cross-Functional Teams: Working with Allies, Enemies, and Other Strangers* (San Francisco: Jossey-Bass, 2003), 166.
4. F. P. Morgeson, M. A. Campion, R. L. Dipboye, J. R. Hollenbeck, K. Murphy, and N. Schmitt, "Are We Getting Fooled Again? Coming to Terms with Limitations in the Use of Personality Tests for Personnel Selection," *Personnel Psychology* 60 (2007): 1029–1049.

4

COMPETENCIES: TEAM SKILLS THAT ARE NEEDED FOR HIGH PERFORMANCE

Once the team context and team composition are created to support team effectiveness, the next step is to develop team competencies. Such competencies are not just the attributes of individual team members but competencies that are developed and shared by members of the team. In this chapter, we discuss the competencies of high-performing teams and provide an assessment tool at the end of the chapter to determine to what extent a team has those competencies.

Developing the Competencies of High-Performing Teams

In this chapter, we describe ten characteristics of high-performing teams:

1. The ability to set clear, measurable goals
2. Making clear team assignments and ensuring that team members are competent to carry out those assignments
3. Using effective decision-making processes
4. Establishing accountability for team members
5. Running effective meetings
6. High trust
7. Creating open communications
8. Managing conflict effectively

9. Creating mutual respect for team members to encourage collaboration

10. Encouraging risk taking and innovation

We will discuss an eleventh competency, change management, in the next chapter.

While these are the competencies that we have found in high-performing teams, each team should identify the set of competencies it will need to achieve success, since certain competencies are more important than others given a team's unique mission and task.

Using our list of ten competencies as a guide, team members should meet and generate a list of the competencies they believe are most important to their success. The team leader should ask, "If we are to become a truly effective team, what competencies do we need to develop together to ensure effective teamwork and collaboration? Let's spend some time now identifying what we think are the most important competencies for our team." The leader could also ask, "What competencies are we already strong in, and which ones do we need to work on?" With the team leader participating but not dominating, the members develop their list.

The purpose of the discussion is to lead to action that will build stronger competencies in the team. This is an important first discussion leading to building team competencies.

Developing Team Guidelines and Metrics to Measure Progress

What guidelines does the team need to become effective according to its own criteria and to avoid pitfalls? Again, with the leader participating but not dominating, the team develops its own set of guidelines. The leader might say, "We need guidelines that will promote open discussion on how we will make decisions and how we will deal with disagreements among team members. We need guidelines on how to ensure that people follow through on assignments. We need clear metrics to know if we are meeting our goals."

These guidelines and metrics should be agreed on by all team members and can be written up and posted for display at all team meetings. Periodically the team should spend some meeting time to consider whether it is following its own guidelines and whether any guidelines need to be added or changed. The "team competency assessment" at the end of this chapter provides some guidance concerning how to measure team competencies.

Developing Team Competencies

Each team needs to determine what competencies are important for success and create a process to discuss and practice these competencies. In this section, we will briefly discuss some of the important issues surrounding the development of each of the ten competencies.

Competency 1: Setting Clear, Measurable Goals

High-performing teams develop the competency to set clear and measurable goals to which all team members are highly committed. Clear goals are those that are *realistic*, *prioritized*, and *measurable*. As the team discusses its goals, it should always try to make sure that the goals are realistic (even though they may be stretch goals) and measurable (otherwise the team has no way of knowing whether it is achieving its goals). The team must be careful not to have too many goals. If it has multiple goals, it should make sure the goals are prioritized so that everyone knows which goals are the most important.

A problem that many teams experience is a lack of commitment to the team goals because they are made by the team leader and just handed to the team. When team members participate in setting the team goals, as well as in how they will be measured, their commitment to those goals increases substantially. We find some team leaders setting unrealistic goals for the team because they say, "If I set goals that are very high, then I'll still be happy if they achieve only seventy-five percent of the goals that I set." We find this approach, in general, is not helpful since the goals are not realistic nor typically accepted by the team. The team leader then is seen as being disingenuous in the process, which can undermine trust and commitment in the team.

Setting Stretch Goals to Motivate Team Performance

Nike's Breaking2 project—designed to break the two-hour barrier for the marathon—offers an excellent illustration of the power of setting stretch goals as a team. In the summer of 2014, Matt Nurse, head of Nike Sports Research Laboratory (NSRL), felt that he and his colleagues were playing it safe. He wanted to push his running shoe design team to devote themselves to something at which they could either succeed or fail definitively. So he asked them to imagine how they would make a two-hour marathon a reality. The fastest the marathon had ever been run was 2:02:57; a sub-two-hour marathon would require almost a 3 minute (2.4%) improvement, which might sound small but represents a giant leap in human performance. "We keep talking about the sub-two," Nurse recalls saying. "It's time to stop talking about it and actually do it."

Sandy Bodecker, VP of special projects, took the challenge to heart—so much so that he signaled his personal commitment to Breaking2 by having 1:59:59 tattooed on his wrist. Bodecker pulled together a diverse team of experts in design, engineering, materials, nutrition, physiology, plus three of the world's fastest marathoners, including Eliud Kipchoge, winner of the Rio Olympics and the world's fastest marathoner. Then they set a deadline for the stretch goal: run a sub-two-hour marathon at the Monza auto track in Italy (chosen for its optimal running and weather conditions) in two years. The designers' goal was to develop the lightest shoes possible while providing cushion and a design that would propel the body forward. They tested design after design with the three marathoners. They finally hit on a design with a carbon-fiber plate in the midsole, which stores and releases energy with each stride and acts as a kind of slingshot to propel runners forward. They also designed lightweight performance clothing to minimize drag.

Then on May 6, 2017, they held a much publicized running event which turned out to be a PR coup, as everyone in the running world watched to see whether Kipchoge could break the two-hour marathon. During the first 15, 17, and even 22 miles, Kipchoge was right behind the two-hour pace car. But during the final two miles, he slowed slightly, finishing in a world record 2:00:25 (it was unofficial because they used other runners, called pacemakers, throughout the race to break the wind and push Kipchoge; but one year later Kipchoge officially broke the world record by more than a minute). Ultimately, the project came up short of its goal. But the shoe that the team developed, the Nike Zoom Vaporfly 4%, and the PR that came with it, was a huge success. "I love the ambition of trying to make history," Nike CEO Mark Parker told us when discussing Breaking2. "When you commit to a stretch goal like that, the whole process can be incredibly uplifting for a team."[1]

Competency 2: Making Assignments Clear and Ensuring Competence

Once clear goals are set, the team then must have a process for making individual assignments so that everyone knows exactly what they are supposed to do and how their work contributes to the team goals. This means clearly documenting who is to do what and by when. It also means identifying the skills and resources each team member needs to fulfill his or her assignment. In some cases, the team roles may need to be codified by creating job descriptions for each team member that are then shared within the team.

There is nothing more frustrating than to be given an assignment that you don't have the skills or resources to complete successfully. Sometimes this may require that certain team members get additional training or that someone from another part of the company (or even from outside the company) is brought in to help complete the assignments. But effective teams develop a process for making clear assignments and then making sure that the team has the skills and resources to complete those tasks. Moreover, team members should know how their work relates to the work of others on the team so they can coordinate their efforts when needed.

Competency 3: Using Effective Decision-Making Processes

Making effective decisions that have the commitment of all team members is another key competency. Teams must make a wide range of decisions—about goals, programs, use of resources, assignments, schedules, and so forth. It should be made clear that in an effective team, not all decisions are made by unanimous consent. In fact, at Amazon one of the core leadership principles is "Have backbone, disagree, and commit. Leaders are obligated to respectfully challenge decisions when they disagree, even when doing so is uncomfortable or exhausting. Leaders have conviction and are tenacious. They do not compromise for the sake of social cohesion. Once a decision is determined, they commit wholly." The point is that team members should be willing to respectfully disagree but all team members should agree that the decision made is one they understand and can implement, even if it is not necessarily their first choice.

As research on decision making shows, sometimes team leaders should make decisions by themselves, sometimes they should consult with team members before making a decision, and sometimes they should let the team make the decision by consensus. The mode of decision making used depends on how critical the decision is, whether the leader has all the data, and whether the team's commitment will be affected if the leader makes the decision alone. If the acceptance of the decision by the team is critical to implementing the decision, then the leader should involve team members in the decision. Moreover, if the team leader doesn't have enough information to make a decision, getting team input is important. However, in cases where the leader has all the information needed to make a decision and acceptance of the decision by the team is assured, then the leader can make the decision without involving the team.

These various decision methods need to be discussed, the key decisions identified, and agreement reached on the decision-making process to be used for each type of decision. A team exercise on decision making is useful for practicing decision-making skills in this phase of team development.

Competency 4: Establishing Accountability for High Performance

High-performance teams encourage high-performance standards, and team members hold each other accountable for performance. Once individual assignments are made, the team needs a process for periodically checking up on team members and holding them accountable for fulfilling their assignments in a way that is acceptable to the team. This might be done either through a one-on-one interview by each team member with the team leader or in a team meeting where team members share their progress with each other in achieving their goals.

Most of us know how frustrating it is to work on a team where people are lazy or shirk their duties. When team members are not held accountable for their work, it demoralizes the entire team. *After all*, they may think, *why should I work hard to achieve team goals when we aren't going to reach them since so-and-so isn't going to do his part?* On effective teams, team members hold each other mutually accountable for team performance—it's not just the team leader's job. This is something we see on successful sports teams: players hold each other mutually accountable for performance and do not expect that to be solely the job of the coach. Sports teams are known for having "players only" meetings to clear the air, identify problems, and clarify accountability without the coach present.

Competency 5: Running Effective Meetings

The team also needs to be competent in running meetings. The general approach to effective meeting management has the following steps:

1. Set out a clear purpose and goal for each meeting.
2. Develop an agenda before the meeting and send it to team members. Team members can then come to the meeting prepared.

3. Structure the items on the agenda to follow a logical sequence. Given time constraints that are usually present, the team may need to put time limits on certain items to make sure all the important issues are discussed.

4. Identify when the discussion is moving off the subject and into areas unrelated to the goals of the meeting. The team can then bring the discussion back to focus on the important issues.

5. Summarize and record the actions, decisions, and assignments made at the meeting and disseminate them to team members after the meeting, usually by e-mail. The team then can follow up to ensure that the meeting's objectives are achieved and assignments are carried out.

6. Make it clear that all team members have the responsibility (and obligation) to call for a meeting if the meeting will help improve the team's performance. The team leader is not solely responsible for initiating team meetings.

By following these simple steps of effective meeting management, a team is more likely to be productive. To train teams in effective meeting management, we have often shown the training video *Meetings, Bloody Meetings*, produced by the Monty Python comedy group, which illustrates the differences between effective and ineffective meetings.[2] A strategy we have also found effective is simply video-recording a meeting and then watching it together (sped up somewhat!) to see how the meeting could have been improved. It may seem like a lot of time to re-watch a meeting, but in the long run it can save you significantly more time than you spend on this one activity.

Competency 6: Building Trust

One of the most important team competencies is trust—trusting others and being worthy of their trust. This is sometimes referred to as creating psychological safety within the team so that team members are willing to express opinions, acknowledge mistakes, and have confidence that they can engage in risky, learning-related behaviors without punishment. The fundamental emotional condition in a team is not "liking" but "trusting."

People do not need to like one another as friends to be able to work together, but they do need to trust one another. Thus, each team member must be both trustworthy and trusting of others, assuming the others are also trustworthy. Being trustworthy means keeping confidences; carrying out assignments and following through on promises and commitments; supporting others when they need support; giving both honest, positive feedback and helpful constructive feedback; being present at team meetings; and being available to help other team members.

If trust among team members has been low, this issue needs to be aired in the team meeting. Trust on the team will increase if specific trustworthy and untrustworthy behaviors are identified and all team members verbally commit themselves to being trustworthy and trusting others. Some teams have developed a guideline for amnesty; team members will grant amnesty for all past behaviors and will respond only to current and future behaviors of others they may have previously distrusted. The amnesty guideline indicates that a team member who feels that another has behaved in an untrustworthy way will go to that person and say, "I could be wrong, but I have felt that you were not as trustworthy as I thought was appropriate. Could we talk about this?" These encounters are sensitive and delicate, and the hope is that the matter can be discussed without either party becoming defensive or belligerent. Sometimes a third party can help to mediate this discussion.

The key to developing trust in a team is to make agreements and then follow through on those agreements. Actions speak louder than words. We often find teams that build trust relatively quickly by making commitments to short-term objectives and following through to meet those commitments. However, we have also found that trust can be lost quickly when the leader or team member fails to meet a commitment. Trust typically takes a long time to build and can be lost quickly. Thus, it is important for the team to ask and discuss the following questions:

- What is the current level of trust in the team?
- What specific actions and commitments need to be made to increase trust?
- How will the team hold its members accountable for their commitments?
- What should we do when someone on the team fails to keep a commitment and trust is undermined?
- What should be our process for regaining trust in the team and the members?

There are three types of trust that need to be managed by the team: interpersonal trust, competence trust, and institutional trust. As we have discussed, *interpersonal trust* can be restored when team members communicate why trust has been lost between them, are willing to change their behaviors, and are willing to be held accountable for making those changes.

Competence trust is lost because team members don't believe that some team members have the skills and experience to help the team succeed and achieve its goals. In such cases, the team needs to help the team member who lacks certain skills to put together a plan to develop the skills needed to help the team. Otherwise, it might make more sense to drop that person from the team.

Institutional trust in the team, not just among individual members, is also an important factor. Having institutional trust means that team members believe that "the team" will treat them fairly and will share relevant information that they need to do their jobs. Transparency—openly sharing information about the team, the organization, and other factors related to team performance—is generally key to creating trust in the team as a whole. Institutional trust is also built when the team follows through on the agreements that have been made with team members. The team leader is generally responsible for building institutional trust in the team.

Competency 7: Establishing Open Communication Channels

Another important competency is open communications. This involves some risk if the norm has been to keep quiet and say only what you think the boss wants to hear. It is helpful if the team leader, consistent with the team philosophy, can say, "I honestly want every person to speak up and share his or her thinking, regardless of whether it is in agreement." As part of the educative phase in competency development for the team, the leader can initiate a team-oriented exercise so that the team has a chance to practice being open, making decisions, testing the trust level, and observing the leader's behavior.[3] The team then has an opportunity to critique its performance after the conclusion of the exercise. A consultant or human resource managers might introduce team leaders to various communications exercises to give them some experience in how to administer and use them.

A natural extension of open communications is giving and receiving feedback. Some guidelines of effective feedback should be discussed. For example, feedback is best given if it is asked for rather than unsolicited. Feedback is more easily accepted if given in the form of a suggestion, for example, "I think you would be more effective if you asked a number of people for their ideas rather than just one or two."

Feedback can also be more effective when given as "descriptive feedback," meaning that you describe behaviors without assigning motives or judgments to those behaviors. For example, saying "You seem to only call on John, Peter, and George when you ask for input from the team" is easier to hear than, "I think you play favorites and listen only to people you like." The latter, where you assign motives to the person is called "evaluative feedback" and is not as helpful as it puts the person on the defensive regarding motives or intentions rather than focusing on the behavior that needs to change.

And don't forget that feedback shouldn't always been seen as a negative thing. Feedback should also be positive: people need to hear what they do well just as much as what they need to improve. Reinforcing positive behavior is just as important as correcting negative behavior.

Sometimes corrective feedback needs to be shared in the team setting if, for example, a person's behavior is blocking the group. Sometimes, however, it is best if the feedback is solicited and/or given in a one-on-one situation. If a person giving feedback feels uncertain, it can be useful to express that uncertainty: "John, I have a dilemma. I have some feedback I think would be useful to you, but I am reluctant to share it with you for fear it might disrupt our relationship. I value our relationship, and it is more important than giving the feedback. How do you think I should deal with this dilemma?" Given this context, the person usually will ask for the feedback to be shared.

Competency 8: Managing Conflict

Effective teams learn how to give and receive constructive feedback (as opposed to critical feedback) without becoming defensive or combative. This is an important competency because continuous improvement requires that team members frequently give and receive constructive feedback so that change is possible. However, when team members give feedback to each other, conflict often results.

Every team has conflicts, and unresolved conflict can destroy a team's ability to function. For this reason, managing conflict effectively is a critical competency. In ineffective teams, conflicts are not discussed openly nor resolved. Moreover, conflict as a result of personal differences or personalities, versus a conflict of ideas, is almost always unhealthy and leads to poor results. As a result of team conflict, much team effort is expended in having offline conversations about the unresolved conflict, and people don't focus on their tasks.

Most conflict is the result of unmet expectations on the part of team members. For example, one team member might feel it's her job to make key decisions regarding meeting agendas while another team member might feel that agenda management is his role. The basic process for resolving such conflicts is as follows:

1. Identify the source of the conflict. This is done by having team members describe their expectations related to the conflicts that they are having. The team leader should manage this process, often playing the role of mediator to clarify the issues and manage some of the emotions that might accompany such a discussion. In some cases, an experienced mediator—often someone from human resources—may be needed to intervene to help the parties work through the issues that divide them.

2. Identify alternative expectations or behaviors that would reduce or eliminate the conflict.

3. Have the team members who are in conflict agree on a course of action to remedy the conflict. Such actions along with a timetable might be put in writing so there will be no ambiguity and people will be reminded what they've committed to do.

4. Regularly follow up in team meetings or in meetings between those in conflict along with the team leader or mediator to track progress related to resolving the conflict.

We have found that such a process is essential for teams to overcome unproductive conflict and enhance team performance. However, if the conflict is personality related or related to some deeper issues that are not easily resolved, removing the problematic team member from the team may be the best solution.

Competency 9: Creating Mutual Respect and Collaboration

Another competency of effective teams is that they know how to collaborate in a spirit of cooperation and mutual respect. This requires that team members understand the need to collaborate and understand that they are each better off if they all help each other.

High-performing teams develop a norm of reciprocity that involves quickly helping each other when asked. This works only when team members develop a healthy mutual respect for each other's skills, learn to care about each other as individuals, and realize that they are truly better off if they collaborate.

We have found that teams that recognize team members who cooperate and help others is a good way to encourage this competency. Rather than just focus on individual achievement, teams can recognize "good citizens" on the team who work to make the team better and don't always focus on their own interests.

Competency 10: Encouraging Risk Taking and Innovation

We have found that team members in high-performing teams are willing to take risks and encourage innovation to help make their teams better. Unfortunately, most teams tend to put down or punish team members who come up with new ways of working together or new solutions to old problems. "We have always done it that way. Why change?" is heard too often in those teams that we've worked with.

To encourage risk taking, the team leader needs to describe to the team the kinds of behaviors that should be rewarded—for example, sharing with the team new approaches to making decisions, providing the team with information about how to run effective meetings, or identifying for the team roadblocks to the team's performance. Then the team leader, while encouraging such behaviors, also needs to clearly and explicitly praise and reward team members when they engage in such behaviors to improve the team. Of course, the team leader should help team members recognize when risk taking is appropriate—after careful thought, planning, and collaboration—versus risks based on sloppy thinking and poor planning. Team members also should be praised for "thoughtful failures," since taking risks inevitably leads to some failures. If the team leader rewards only successful risks, little risk taking will take place.

Task and Relationship Competencies

To be successful at building an effective team, it is useful if the team can understand that all groups function and develop competencies at two levels: (1) a task level, at which people are trying to set goals, make assignments and decisions, and get work done; and (2) a relationship level, at which people are dealing with one another's feelings and ongoing relationships. At the task level, teams need people to proffer ideas and suggestions, evaluate ideas, make decisions and assignments, and allocate resources. At the relationship level, team members need to support and encourage one another, invite more hesitant members to contribute, ease tension and provide some humor (without disrupting the task), and generally provide group maintenance, just as one would engage in the maintenance of a piece of machinery.

Successful teams show a concern for getting the task done but also a concern for managing relationships and always need to balance these concerns. Sometimes it is easy to become so worried about completing the tasks and getting the work done that relationships are trampled on, and other times it is necessary to get down to work and spend less time being concerned about relationships. Team members should be aware of actions and behaviors that block the team at either of these two levels and at least be able to say, "I think we are getting bogged down on nonwork activities and need to move ahead on our work," or, "I think we have lost the participation of two members, and I would like to stop and see how they are feeling about what we are doing." Such actions could occur during the team meeting or might be shared during the critiquing session at the end. More specific guidance about managing change will be discussed in the next chapter.

Helping teams develop these important competencies and creating the opportunity to practice them should be part of any team development program. To develop team competencies team leaders need to be prepared so they can educate the team on how to develop the competencies we have discussed in this chapter. However, a support or human resource person may also be needed to help manage this process in collaboration with the team leader if the team leader lacks experience or is uncertain how to proceed in helping the team develop these importance competencies.

Measurement of Team Competencies

The Team Competencies Scale below is a team assessment tool that can be used by a team to examine its processes to see what level of competence it has achieved. Members of the team should fill out the scale, compute an average for the total team, and identify which areas they believe need improvement.

Team Competencies Scale for Assessment

Instructions: Using your observations of your work unit, evaluate the maturity of your team by answering the following questions on a scale of 1 (a less competent or immature team) to 5 (a mature, competent team).

Team Competency 1: Setting Clear, Measurable Goals

1. Does the team know how to set clear, measurable goals?

1	2	3	4	5
Team goals are unclear, and team performance is not measured.		Team goals are somewhat clear and occasionally measured.		The team effectively sets clear goals and tracks performance.

---

2. Does the team develop commitment within team members to achieve team goals?

1	2	3	4	5
People demonstrate surface-level commitment to the goals.		People work at achieving only the goals with which they agree.		Everyone is deeply committed to all of the goals.

Team Competency 2: Making Assignments Clear and Ensuring Competence

3. Does the team make assignments that all team members clearly understand?

1	2	3	4	5
People are often confused about their assignments and how they relate to others' work.		Team members are occasionally confused about their assignments and how they contribute to team performance.		Each team member clearly understands his or her assignment and how it contributes to team performance.

(Continued)

4. Does the team know how to develop the skills in team members to accomplish their assignments?

1	2	3	4	5
Team members lack skills, and there is no plan to help them develop the skills necessary to complete their assignments.		There is some effort to develop team members' skills.		The team regularly assesses individual skills and develops plans to improve the skills of individual team members.

Team Competency 3: Using Effective Decision-Making Processes

5. Does the team know how to make decisions effectively?

1	2	3	4	5
The team has no processes for making decisions. The boss tells us what the decisions are.		The team has some processes for decision making, but there is often confusion as to how decisions are made.		The team has clear processes for making decisions and knows how and when to use consensus decision making.

6. To what extent do people appropriately participate in, accept, and implement decisions with commitment?

1	2	3	4	5
There is often a failure to involve people in decision making. There is little personal commitment to decisions.		At times, there is some involvement and commitment to decisions; at other times, there is not.		There is appropriate participation and full commitment by everyone to all decisions.

Team Competency 4: Establishing Accountability for High Performance

7. Does the team encourage high-performance standards and hold team members accountable?

1	2	3	4	5
There is little encouragement of high performance. Team members are not held accountable.		There is some accountability and encouragement of high performance.		Team members set high performance standards and hold each other accountable.

(Continued)

Team Competency 5: Running Effective Meetings

8. Does the team run effective meetings?

1	2	3	4	5
Meetings are ineffective; there is little preparation, no clear agenda, and little follow-through on decisions made.		Meetings are somewhat effective.		Meetings are very effective. There is significant preparation; agendas are well organized, and the team follows through on decisions made at the meeting.

Team Competency 6: Building Trust

9. Does the team know how to build trust among team members?

1	2	3	4	5
There is almost no trust. Team members don't follow through on promises and commitments.		Some trust exists, but it is not widespread.		There is high trust among all team members. Everyone follows through on promises and commitments.

Team Competency 7: Establishing Open Communication Channels

10. How would you describe the team leader's management style?

1	2	3	4	5
She or he is authoritarian and runs things his or her way without listening to others.		She or he is somewhat consultative; consults with us but makes the final decision.		She or he is participative; is part of the team and willing to listen and be influenced.

11. Does the team know how to foster open and free communication?

1	2	3	4	5
Communication is very closed, guarded, and careful; information is not shared.		Communication is somewhat open; people will talk only about matters that are safe.		Communication is very open and information is shared; everyone feels free to say what he or she wants.

(Continued)

Team Competency 8: Managing Conflict

12. Does the team know how to manage conflict effectively?

1	2	3	4	5
Conflicts are ignored, or people are told not to worry about them.		Conflicts are sometimes looked at but are usually left hanging.		Conflicts are discussed openly and resolved.

13. Does the team know how to give and receive feedback without becoming defensive or combative?

1	2	3	4	5
No, information and feedback are not shared. If given, the feedback is not constructive or makes people defensive.		Yes, some information is shared, and constructive feedback is given without people becoming too defensive.		Yes, information is shared, and feedback is clear, timely, and helpful. Team members welcome feedback without becoming defensive.

Team Competency 9: Creating Mutual Respect and Collaboration

14. How well do team members collaborate with others?

1	2	3	4	5
Each person works independent of others without recognizing the need to collaborate.		There is some collaboration when people are pushed to it.		People quickly offer to help each other on assignments; they easily work with others as needed.

15. How supportive and helpful are the team leader and members toward one another?

1	2	3	4	5
There is little cooperation and support; team members don't help each other.		There is some cooperation and support; team members help each other some of the time.		There is a high degree of cooperation and support; team members always help each other.

(Continued)

Team Competency 10: Engaging in Risk Taking and Innovation

16. Are people willing to take a risk and try out new actions to make the team better?

1	2	3	4	5
No one is willing to take risks or bring new ideas to the team. Risk takers are often punished.		There is some willingness to take risks and bring new ideas to the team.		There is a high willingness to take risks and bring new ideas to the team.

Scoring: Each person should add up his or her score for the 16 items and divide that total by 16. This will give the competency score of the team as perceived by that member. If you add up all of the individual scores and divide by the number of members of the team, you will find the team's rating of its competence.

If the ratings are 3.75 or higher, there is an appropriate level of competence.

If the scores are between 2.5 and 3.75, competency is at a midlevel, with work still to be done by the team and team leader.

If the score is between 1.00 and 2.50, the team is at an immature or low competency level, and a great deal of team building is needed.

An item analysis, that is, looking at the individual and team scores for each item, will help the team see the areas that need the most work to move the team to a higher level of competence.

Notes

1. https://www.wired.com/story/nike-breaking2-marathon-eliud-kipchoge/.
2. *Meetings, Bloody Meetings* (Chicago: Video Arts, 1994), videotape.
3. For examples of such exercises, see D. L. Anderson, *Organization Development: The Process of Leading Organizational Change*, 2nd ed. (Thousand Oaks, CA: Sage, 2012).

5

CHANGE MANAGEMENT: HOW EFFECTIVE TEAMS IMPROVE THEIR PERFORMANCE

The fourth C refers to change, the key meta-competency in our model. High-performing teams are not only aware of what is impeding their performance but are able to take corrective action to solve their problems and achieve their goals. In this chapter, we discuss (1) the common problems found in teams and how to diagnose them, (2) how to determine whether the team itself can solve its problems or whether a facilitator or consultant is needed, and (3) the basic elements of programs designed to initiate change within the team. In Chapter 7 we will discuss in greater detail how organizations can put together team-building programs that are organization-wide.

Common Problems Found in Teams

Usually a team-building program is undertaken when a concern, problem, issue, or set of symptoms leads the manager or other members of the team to believe that the effectiveness of the team is not what it could be. The following symptoms or conditions usually provoke serious thought or remedial action:

- Failure to achieve team goals
- A reduction in productivity
- Unexplained increase in costs
- Increases in grievances or complaints from team members
- Complaints from clients about quality of the product or service
- Conflict among team members

- Confusion about assignments
- Lack of broad team support for decisions
- Decisions not carried out properly—lack of follow-through
- Apathy and general lack of interest or involvement of team members
- Lack of initiative, imagination, or innovation
- Ineffective meetings
- Problems with the team leader—high dependence on or negative reactions to the team leader
- Poor communication (people not speaking up or not listening to each other)

Most of these are symptoms; that is, they result from or are caused by other underlying factors that are the root causes of the problems. A loss of productivity, for example, might be caused by such factors as conflicts between team members or problems with the team leader. The following survey is one way to assess how a team is performing.

Team-Building Checklist

Problem identification: To what extent is there evidence of the following problems in your team? Circle the number that best represents your opinion.

	Low Evidence		Some Evidence		High Evidence
Failure to achieve team goals	1	2	3	4	5
Loss of productivity	1	2	3	4	5
Unexplained increase in costs	1	2	3	4	5
Grievances or complaints within the team	1	2	3	4	5

	Low Evidence		Some Evidence		High Evidence
Complaints from clients about team performance	1	2	3	4	5
Conflict among team members	1	2	3	4	5
Confusion about assignments	1	2	3	4	5
Poor decision making	1	2	3	4	5
Decisions not being carried out properly	1	2	3	4	5
Apathy or general lack of interest or involvement of team members	1	2	3	4	5
Lack of innovation, risk taking, imagination, or initiative	1	2	3	4	5
Ineffective meetings	1	2	3	4	5
Problems in working with the team leader	1	2	3	4	5
Poor communications: people afraid to speak up, not listening to one another	1	2	3	4	5

Scoring: Add up the score for the 14 items.

If the team's score is between 14 and 28, the team is functioning at a high level.

If the score is between 29 and 42, there is some evidence that team development is needed.

If the score is between 42 and 56, the team has a number of problems and is in need of change.

If the score is over 56, team building should be a top priority for the team.

In some instances the team leader or other members of the team may not have the skills or experience to launch a team-building program. If that is recognized by the team leader and the team, an outside facilitator or consultant may be needed to help the team improve its performance. The following checklist provides some guidance concerning whether an outside person is needed to help the team with its efforts to manage change.

Do You Need a Consultant for Team Building?

Directions: Answer the following questions by responding either "yes," "no," or "don't know." Circle the appropriate response.

Does the team leader feel comfortable in trying out something new and different with the team?	Yes	No	Don't know
Does the team have prior positive experiences working through difficult issues when team members have different views?	Yes	No	Don't know
Will team members speak up and be honest?	Yes	No	Don't know
Does your team generally work together without a lot of conflict?	Yes	No	Don't know
Are you reasonably sure that the team leader is not a major source of difficulty?	Yes	No	Don't know
Is there high commitment by the leader and team members to achieve more effective team functioning?	Yes	No	Don't know
Is the personal style of the leader and his or her management philosophy consistent with a team approach?	Yes	No	Don't know
Do you feel your team can effectively run a team-building program without help?	Yes	No	Don't know

> *Scoring:* **If there are six or more "yes" responses,** the team prob-ably does not need an outside consultant. **If there are four or more "no" responses,** a consultant is probably needed. **If there are a mix-ture of "yes," "no," and "don't know" responses,** the team leader should discuss the situation with a consultant and make a joint deci-sion regarding the consultant's involvement with the team.

Team Building as a Process

Many people think of "team building" as a one-time fun retreat. They imagine the team going somewhere remote to do "trust falls" and other bonding activities, then returning to work and conducting business as usual. Those who think about team building in this way generally see no long-term success. Team building should be thought of as an ongoing process, not as a single event. Some organizations actually institutionalize team development as part of their ongoing activities. For example, Bain & Company does team building on a monthly basis to ensure that team problems are quickly identified and resolved.

The ability for a team to be aware of its strengths and weak-nesses and then take action to improve its performance is a "meta-competency" that great teams have. This ability allows them to systematically evaluate and change the way the team functions. This means changing team processes, values, team member skillsets, reward systems, or even the resources available to get teamwork done. The philosophy one should have about team development is the same as the philosophy behind what the Japanese call *kaizen,* or continuous improvement: the job is never done because there are always new bottlenecks preventing even better team performance.

The team development process often starts with a block of time devoted to helping the group look at its current level of functioning and to devise more effective ways of working together. In fact, one approach to doing this is to follow the *kaizen* approach and have the team identify the biggest bottleneck to improved team performance and then develop a plan to address and fix that bottleneck. This ini-tial sequence of data sharing, diagnosis, and action planning takes time and should not be crammed into a couple of hours. Ideally the members of the team should plan to meet for at least one half day, one full day, or even two days, for the initial program. A common format is to meet for dinner, have an evening session, and then meet all the next day or for whatever length of time has been set aside.

This meeting is not to focus on *what* the team will do, but *how* the team will do it. This is sometimes difficult because oftentimes people want to dive right into getting the work done, not realizing that they will accomplish much more if the team has established how they will get it done. For this reason, it is customary to hold the initial team development program away from the work site. The argument for this is that if people meet at the work location, they will find it difficult to ignore their day-to-day concerns in order to concentrate fully on the goals of the program. Thus, most team-building facilitators recommend having team development programs at a location where they can have people's full time and attention.

Most team-building facilitators also prefer to have a longer block of time (even up to three days) to get the team engaged and really make progress in establishing a team development program. Of course, this may not be practical in some situations. Since we are thinking of team development as an ongoing process, it is possible to start with shorter amounts of time regularly scheduled over a period of several weeks. Some teams have successfully conducted a program that opened with an evening meeting followed by a two-to-four-hour meeting each week for the next several weeks. Commitment to the process, regular attendance, high involvement, and good use of time are all more important than length of time.

Use of an Outside Facilitator or Consultant

Team leaders often ask, "Should I conduct the team development effort on my own, or should I get an outside person to help us?" As we noted previously, an "outside person" can mean a consultant from outside the organization or an internal consultant who is employed by the organization, often in human resources or organization development and with a background in team development.

Ultimately the team leader is responsible for team development. This is an important concept to remember. Some team leaders think that by bringing in an outside consultant they no longer have primary responsibility for the development of the team. However, the consultant should be seen as assisting the team leader and the team, not as replacing the leader's responsibility to lead the team. The consultant's job is to get the process started and to be a neutral "sounding board" for the team leader and team members. The use of a consultant is generally advisable if a manager is aware of problems, feels that he or she may be one of those problems, and is not sure exactly what to do or how to do it but feels strongly enough that some positive action is necessary to pull the team together to improve performance.

The Roles of Team Leader and Consultant

Ultimately the team leader or manager is responsible to develop a productive team and develop processes that will allow the team to regularly stop and critique itself and plan for its improvement. It is the leader's responsibility to keep a finger on the pulse of his or her team and plan appropriate actions if the team shows signs of stress, ineffectiveness, or operating difficulty.

Unfortunately, many team leaders and managers have not been trained to do the data gathering, diagnosis, and planning and take the actions required to maintain and improve their teams. The role of the consultant is to work with the manager until the manager is capable of incorporating team development activities as a regular part of his or her managerial responsibilities. The manager and the consultant (whether external or internal) should form their own two-person team in working through the initial team-building program. In all cases, the manager or team leader will be responsible for all team-building activities, although he or she may use the consultant as a resource. The goal of the consultant's work is to leave the leader capable of continuing team development without the assistance of the consultant or with minimal help.

The Team-Building Cycle

Ordinarily a team-building program follows a cycle similar to that depicted in Figure 5.1. The team-building cycle typically begins when someone recognizes one or more problems that should be addressed by the team. After identifying the problem the next step is to gather data to determine the root causes. The data are then analyzed and a diagnosis is made. After the diagnosis, the team engages in appropriate planning and problem solving. Actions are planned and assignments made. The plans are put into action and the results honestly evaluated.

Sometimes there is no clear, obvious problem. The concern is then to identify or find the problems that may be present but hidden along with their underlying causes. The team leader must continue to gather and analyze the data, identify the problems and the causes, and then move to action planning. Team members work together to carry out the program from the time the problem has been identified

Figure 5.1 The Team-Building Cycle

through some form of evaluation. This process then iterates until the problem has been resolved.

We'll now address, in more detail, the steps in the team-building cycle.

Data Gathering

Because team building encourages a team to do its own problem solving, and given that a critical condition for effective problem solving is accurate data, it is extremely important to gather valid data on the hypothesized causes behind the symptoms or problems originally identified. A consultant initially may assist in the data gathering, but eventually a team should develop the ability to collect its own data as a basis for working on its own problems. The consultant should be part of the data gathering to ensure that the methods of gathering data aren't biased toward one point of view or one solution. In cases where trust is low in the team and data gathered by other team members may be viewed with suspicion, the consultant may need to collect all the data for the team. The following are some common data-gathering methods.

Surveys One of the most common approaches to gathering data is to conduct a survey of all team members. Surveys are helpful when there are relatively large numbers of team members or members would be more open in responding to an anonymous survey. It also can be helpful to use a survey if you want to compare the issues and problems facing different teams in an organization.

There are two general types of surveys: open- and closed-ended surveys. An open-ended survey asks questions such as: What do you like about your team? What problems does your team need to address? and What suggestions do you have to improve the team? Team members can give their responses in writing. The team leader or consultant summarizes these responses and presents them to the team in a team-building session. It may be somewhat messy to summarize such raw data, but it often helps to read the actual views of the team members to better understand the issues and how the members are feeling.

Closed-ended surveys force the person responding to choose a specific response. Most of the surveys in this book are closed-ended (but often with one or two open-ended questions at the end). Closed-ended surveys make tabulating the results easy and statistical comparisons possible. However, they may miss some of the important dynamics and problems of a team. Closed-ended surveys are a useful starting point, however, to create awareness of the problems facing a team and begin a discussion of how to solve those problems. We have found that the team-building checklist in this chapter and the Team Context (see Chapter 2), Team Composition (see Chapter 3) and Team Competencies (see Chapter 4) scales are helpful surveys to gather data about a team.

Interviews At times a consultant can perform a useful service by interviewing the members of the team. The manager or team leader could conduct such interviews, but in most cases, team members will be more open in sharing data with someone from outside the team. The consultant tries to determine the causes behind the problem in order to pinpoint those conditions that may need to be changed or improved. In these interviews the consultant often asks the following questions:

1. Why is this team having the kinds of problems it has?
2. What keeps you personally from being as effective as you would like to be?
3. What things do you like best about the team?
4. What changes would make the team more effective?
5. How could this team begin to work more effectively together?

Following the interviews, the consultant frequently does a content analysis of the interviews, identifies the major themes or suggestions that emerge, and prepares a summary presentation.

At the team-building meeting, the consultant presents the summary, and the team, under the leader's direction, analyzes the data and plans actions to deal with the major concerns.

Some consultants prefer not to conduct interviews prior to the team-building meeting and do not want to present a data summary. They have found that information shared in a private interview with a consultant is not as readily discussed in the open, with all other team members present, especially if some of those members have been the object of some of the interview information. Some consultants have painfully discovered that people often deny what they said in the interview, fight the data, and refuse to use what they said as a basis for discussion and planning. At times it may be appropriate for the consultant to interview people privately to understand some of the deeply rooted issues but still have people present their own definitions of the problems in an open session.

One question often arises about interviewing: Should the interviews be kept anonymous so that no one will be identified? We have found that if data are gathered from a team and those data are then presented to that team, team members often can figure out who said what. Keeping sources anonymous is often difficult, if not impossible. Thus, we typically say to a team member before starting an interview: "You will not be personally identified in the summary we present back to the team, but you must be aware that people might recognize you as the source of certain data. Thus, you should respond to the questions with information that you'd be willing to discuss in the team and might possibly be identified with. However, if you have some information that is important for us to know but you don't want it to be reported back, you can give such information 'off the record.' This information won't be reported, but it might prove useful to us to better understand the team's problems." We have found this approach helpful in getting team members to open up and share information with us about the team. It also encourages team members to own their own feelings and be willing to discuss them in the team.

Team Data Gathering An alternative to surveys and interviewing is open data sharing in a team setting. With this method, each person in the team is asked to share his or her views (on a particular problem or issue) publicly with the other team members. The data shared may not be as inclusive as data revealed in an interview, but each person feels responsible to own up to the information he or she presents to the group and to deal with the issue raised. To prevent forced disclosure, one good ground rule is to tell people that they should raise only those issues they feel they can honestly discuss with the others. They then generally present only the information they feel comfortable discussing; thus, the open sharing of data may result in less information but more willingness to "work the data." It may be helpful to systematically discuss barriers to effective team functioning that may exist in the other four Cs: team context, team composition, team competencies, or team leadership.

With a team data gathering format, each person presents his or her views on what keeps the team from being as effective as it could be or suggests reasons for a particular problem. Each person also describes the things he or she likes about the team, hindrances to personal effectiveness, and the changes he or she feels would be helpful. These data are compiled on a flipchart or whiteboard. (In another variation, data for a large team could be gathered and shared in subgroups.) Then the group moves on to the next stage of the team-building cycle, data analysis.

Diagnosis and Analysis of Data

With all the data now available, the manager and the consultant work with the team to summarize the data and put the information into a priority listing. The following summary categories could be used:

A. Issues that we can work on in this meeting.

B. Issues that someone else must work on (and identify who the others would be). For example, context issues, such as changing reward systems, often need to be addressed with people who are not on the team.

C. Issues that apparently are not open to change—that is, things we must learn to accept or live with.

Category A items become the top agenda items for the rest of the team-building session. Category B items are those for which strategies must be developed by involving others. For category C items, the group must develop coping mechanisms. If the manager is prepared, he or she can handle the summary and sort the data into these three categories. If the manager feels uneasy about this, the consultant may function as a role model to show how this is done.

The next important step is to review all the data and try to identify underlying factors that may be related to several problems. A careful analysis of the data may show that certain procedures, rules, or job assignments are causing several disruptive conditions.

Action Planning

After the agenda has been developed out of the data, the roles of the team leader or manager and the consultant diverge. The leader should move directly into the customary role of group leader. The issues identified should become problems to solve and the team leader should lead the team in creating action plans to address the problems.

While the leader conducts the meeting, the consultant functions as a group observer and facilitator. MIT professor Edgar Schein has referred to this activity as "process consulting," a function that others in the group also can learn to perform.[1] In this role, the consultant helps the group look at its problem-solving and work processes. He or she may stop the group if certain task functions or relationship functions are missing or being performed poorly. If the group gets bogged down or steamrolled into uncommitted decisions, the consultant helps the team look at these processes, why they occur, and how to avoid them in the future. In this role, the consultant trains the group to develop better problem-solving skills.

Implementation and Evaluation

If the actions planned at the team-building session are to make any difference, they must be put into practice. Ensuring that plans are implemented has always been a major function of management. The team leader must be committed to the team plans; without commitment, it is unlikely that a leader can effectively hold people responsible for assignments agreed on in the team-building meeting.

The consultant's role is to observe the degree of action during the implementation phase and be particularly active during the evaluation period. Another data-gathering process now begins to evaluate the impact of the team's change program. It is important to see if the actions planned or the goals developed during the team-building sessions have been achieved. Again, this ultimately should be the responsibility of the leader, but the consultant can help train the manager to carry out an effective program evaluation.

The team leader and the consultant should work closely together in any team development effort. It is ineffective for the leader to turn the whole effort over to the consultant with the plea, "You're the expert. Why don't you do it for me?" Such action leads to a great deal of dependence on the consultant, and if the consultant is highly effective, it can cause the leader to feel inadequate or even more dependent. If the consultant is ineffective, the leader can then reject the plans developed as being unworkable or useless, and the failure of the team-building program is blamed on the consultant. Team leaders must take responsibility for the team-building program, and consultants simply help them plan and take action in unfamiliar areas where they may need to develop the skills required to be successful.

The consultant must be honest, aggressively forthright, and sensitive. He or she must be able to help leaders look at their own leadership style and its impact in facilitating or hindering team effectiveness. The consultant needs to help group members get important data out in the open and keep them from feeling threatened for shar-ing with others. The consultant's role involves helping the group develop skills in group problem solving and planning. To do this, the consultant must have a good understanding of group processes and be able to help the group look at its own dynamics. Finally, the consultant's job is to build skills in the team so that the team is able to solve problems independently and no longer needs the help of a consultant.

Note

1. E. H. Schein, *Process Consultation: Its Role in Organization Develop-ment* (Reading, MA: Addison-Wesley, 1988).

6

COLLABORATIVE LEADERSHIP: THE ROLE OF THE TEAM LEADER

The fifth C in our model is *collaborative leadership*. The reason we use the term *collaborative* is because successful team leaders typically need to collaborate with those within the team as well as persons outside the team in order to help the team function effectively. For example, to change the team's performance appraisal systems often requires the team leader to get approval from senior managers and help from human resources. A company's human resource managers typically play an important role in recruiting and training team members as well as helping the team develop competencies to succeed as a team. So the team leader may need to solicit their support. Team leaders may also want advice from outside consultants to help the team manage change effectively. Thus, the team leader needs to be willing to collaborate with a variety of stakeholders who can help the team improve its performance.

In addition to this "collaborator" role, we have found that effective team leaders do the following:[1]

- Articulate a clear vision of the team's goals and the metrics that will accurately measure team performance.
- Set clear direction for the team with regard to how to achieve team goals.
- Motivate and inspire team members as they pursue team goals.
- Teach and coach team members in developing the skills necessary to complete team tasks.
- Help each team member feel that she or he is valued and an important contributor to the team.

- Hold team members accountable for their contributions to team performance.
- Include and listen to team members when making decisions that affect the team.
- Manage conflict and solve team problems effectively.

We find that team leaders often do not receive adequate training for the role of team leader. As a result they are ill equipped to lead the team and have been set up for a potential disaster. Bain & Company has a well-thought-out process for developing and selecting team leaders that ensures competent team leadership. No one at Bain is promoted to be the manager of a team without demonstrating the skill set necessary to be an effective team leader. Each manager may have one or two "case team leaders" who have responsibility for a portion of the team's work and lead the work of perhaps two or three consultants or business analysts. The company has adopted a promotion process that essentially results in the flipside of the Peter Principle.[2] Rather than promoting people to their level of incompetence, Bain requires that prospective managers demonstrate the full complement of managerial skills, and particularly "intellectual leadership," in a "case team leader" role before they are promoted to manager.

Just like any other manager or partner, they receive a monthly evaluation from the team regarding their leadership performance. Over time the company has studied what makes an effective team leader. In the early days in the firm, they found that extraordinary teams (as measured by quantifiable results for the client) were led by team leaders who exhibited great "intellectual leadership." Intellectual leadership might best be defined as the ability to create and communicate a clear vision for the team's client work. Effective managers are able to identify the key client problems that need to be addressed and they excel at laying out a structured problem-solving approach for the team. They also excel at drawing upon their knowledge and experience to brainstorm and generate value-added ideas for the client. The ability to personally solve client problems is at the heart of "intellectual leadership."

However, more recent studies of employee satisfaction at Bain have found that the most effective team leaders are those who "motivate, inspire, and value" their team members. In other words, just being a smart, effective problem solver isn't enough to inspire a team of individuals to work collaboratively—drawing upon their collective knowledge and skills—to generate a value-added solution. Thus, Bain now evaluates and gives roughly equal weight to both intellectual leadership and collaborative leadership. Individuals must demonstrate these skills as a case team leader in order to qualify to be promoted to the position of case team manager. This approach has helped the company develop a core of managers who are generally highly effective at leading productive teams right from the start.

The Changing Roles of Team Leadership

Most managers and supervisors have worked with their subordinates primarily in boss–subordinate relationships. Such relationships typically are based on the assumption that the boss sets the direction and leads, and the subordinate's role is to carry out the directives of the supervisor. From this view of team leadership, team leaders set team goals, make key decisions by themselves, determine team members' assignments, keep information to themselves, and, in general, create a climate within the team that encourages team members to "follow the leader." This leadership style may be appropriate in certain situations where: (1) the task requires little input from team members; (2) the skill level of team members need not be very high to accomplish the task; (3) there is high turnover in the team, requiring managers to provide direction to new team members; and (4) little innovation is needed for the team to be successful. Teams in fast-food restaurants, for example, may need more direction from the leader due to the nature of the work and the high turnover experienced in that industry.

However, we have found that in most situations developing effective teams requires team leaders to think of their subordinates as teammates rather than merely individuals designated to carry out their orders. In such teams, goals are jointly set by team members with team leaders. Decisions are team decisions and assignments are made after consultation between the team leader and team members. While team members support the team leader, feedback—sometimes negative—is shared about the team and the team leader and communications are open and honest. Team leaders also share all relevant information with the team so that the team can make well-informed decisions. Finally, the team as a whole, not just the team leader, feels responsible for the conduct and the performance of the team.

When a team is just forming or when team members are relatively inexperienced or do not have the requisite skills yet to function effectively in the team, the team leader may need to be more directive. However, over time, as the team matures, the team leader's role needs to change from a more directive role to one that is more participative and collaborative. The following discussion outlines how these roles change over time as a team matures.

The Shift from Individual to Team Leadership

If team leaders see their role as one of dominating the team, there will be little, if any, synergy among team members or empowerment of team members. Effective teams are successful because they take advantage of the complementary knowledge and skills of team members: everyone on the team contributes something different to team performance. The team still has a recognized leader, but that person's use of power and definition of the role are very different from an authoritarian leader. The team's leader tends to give more responsibility to the team, opens up lines of communication, encourages collaboration and mutual helping among members, and allows—even encourages—differences of opinion and helps the team work through those differences. At Bain, everyone is taught to follow the mantra: "Listen, Execute, Add Value." Team members should certainly listen and execute on the directions of the leader. But they are encouraged to "add value," meaning that they should provide valued input to the direction of the team and its work product. This is expected if a consultant hopes to be promoted to the next level of responsibility. Thus, effective leaders spend time encouraging the input and ideas from team members so that team members feel responsible for working together to accomplish common goals.

To achieve this shift in leadership style, over time team leaders need to move more power and responsibility to team members and redefine their leadership role. Figure 6.1 shows how power and roles need to shift to change an immature team into an effective team.

In the beginning of team development, the team leader is usually in a traditional leadership role, with a minimal amount of power or authority delegated to subordinates. But to be effective over time, the leader must be helped to see the leadership role as being more collaborative in nature, both with team members and those stakeholders outside of the team. This transition is often very difficult for a team leader who feels more comfortable making the decisions and being in control of the team. Sharing authority and responsibility with the team can create uncertainty and anxiety for the team leader, and thus resistance to this change in role is not uncommon. However, an effective team leader generally sees his or her role changing from initially being an educator, to becoming

Figure 6.1 Team Development Model

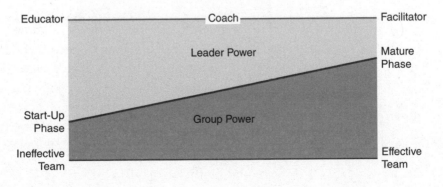

a coach, and eventually moving into the role of a facilitator. We'll discuss each of these roles in turn.

Team Leader as Educator

Assuming that the leader is committed to leading a high-performing team, the first task for the leader in the team development model in Figure 6.1 is to understand how the other 4Cs of team performance are affecting the team and develop a plan to align team context, composition, competencies, and plans for change. This generally requires the team leader to educate the team regarding the 5C model and in particular to help train team members in those competencies that will be needed for the team to function effectively.

While the team needs to be aware of the context and composition issues that may affect the team and be willing to work with the team leader to make needed changes in those areas, most team education programs begin with a focus on team competencies. The team leader should review the ten team competencies we described in Chapter 4 along with the competency of "change management" presented in Chapter 5 and identify with the team those areas where the team needs to improve.

Having team members fill out the team competencies survey in Chapter 4 and sharing the results with the team will help identify those competencies that need attention. For example, if, after taking the survey, meeting management is seen as a problem for the team, then the team could review the best practices related to meeting management outlined in Chapter 4 and then implement those practices in the team. Ideally, the team leader should educate the team members about the key competencies. However, if the leader feels inadequate to conduct these education sessions, an outside facilitator or consultant might be called in to provide assistance. In most companies, the human resources department is a good training resource that team leaders can use to help facilitate training sessions.

In this education phase, the leader:

- Demonstrates a willingness to share power and responsibility with team members

- Encourages team members to become more active in sharing leadership responsibilities
- Develops team performance metrics and guidelines on how the team will function in the future to achieve those performance goals
- Develops with team members the basic competencies of an effective team
- Presents and practices the key competencies that the team needs: being trusting and trustworthy, fostering open communications (sharing all relevant data), giving and receiving feedback, making decisions that have the commitment of all, and observing and critiquing group processes, etc.

Educating the Team

During the education phase of team development, team leaders, in additional to competency training, need to train the team regarding the changing nature of their leadership role. Over time, the team will need to take more responsibility for team functioning and results as the team leader begins to share power with the team. To facilitate this process, the team leader needs to show commitment to a more participative leadership role. This can be done in a variety of ways: asking a team member to build a team meeting agenda by contacting all of the other members for agenda items; allowing a member to chair a team meeting; asking members for their ideas, suggestions, or criticisms of proposals on the table; setting goals and making decisions that require full participation; or delegating significant work to team members without continually checking up on them. Sharing power is the basis of true participative management. Team members must feel that they are partners with the team leader in the work to be done, that their ideas are listened to and respected, and that they can disagree with the team leader without fear of reprisal.

The concept of leadership to be taught and practiced is that leadership is not something located in a position but is instead a *process* that can be shared with others. A person who shares in the leadership process sees an action that is needed to move the team ahead and then has the initiative to take the action. Leadership is truly shared when every team member feels responsible to initiate an action whenever he or she sees the team struggling or getting bogged down. Team members do not wait and say, "If the leader doesn't do something soon, we are going to waste a lot of time and make some very poor decisions." Thus, all team members, not just the leader, feel responsible for improving the functioning of the team.

Team Leader as Coach

As the team matures and the leader shifts more power and responsibility for team functioning from his or her shoulders to the team, the leader's role begins to change from educator to coach. This should not occur until team members understand the team leader's leadership role and have developed some competence in their own leadership skills. Team members also should have experienced the willingness of the team leader to share responsibility and authority with them.

Coaching involves identifying problems facing the team and then helping the team or team member take actions to address that problem and improve performance. It is also a way to reinforce and encourage positive behaviors that the team or an individual exhibits. Coaches must observe and have regular contact with members of their team. Hence, they must be "out with the troops," watching how they perform, critiquing their performance, and providing specific, helpful feedback.

Effective coaches tend to ask questions more than give answers. Certainly coaches may have their own views about what the team should be doing, but they encourage team members to develop their own insights regarding what to do and how to do it. This Socratic method of asking questions helps team members discover what they need to do to help the team succeed and gain insights about how to improve themselves personally. This coaching process helps team members feel empowered and consequently they develop a deeper understanding of the competencies necessary to achieve team excellence. Most important, team members must recognize that the coach's role is to help them succeed—not merely to be a critic or a purveyor of advice. People generally are willing to listen, take advice, and make needed changes if they see the source of such advice as being both authoritative and caring. Thus, the team leader needs to be seen as a knowledgeable helper or mentor in order to function effectively.

One of the mistakes a leader can make is to move too quickly and start to coach when the team has not been adequately educated. If the leader starts to make decisions by consensus and the team members do not understand what consensus is, they could be confused by and suspicious of the leader's behavior. But if they understand the role of the leader as coach, the team generally comes to accept and welcome this leadership style. Sometimes coaching is best done with the whole team present, reviewing again the guidelines for consensus or for critiquing group processes. But sometimes coaching is most appropriate for a particular team member in a private session.

Team Leader as Facilitator

In this final phase in making the transition to a high-performing team, the leader functions as a facilitator. The leader's primary role is to intervene in the team's actions only when attention needs to be focused on a matter the team is having a problem with. Like coaches, facilitators often get more mileage out of asking questions than giving answers. Thus, the leader as facilitator might say, "It seems to me that a vote is being taken before everyone has been able to speak. Do you see the same things I do?" Or the leader might intervene by saying, "If we move ahead in this direction, will this really get us to the overall mission or goals we have set? Have we reached a real or a false consensus? Does everyone feel satisfied with the way we have been functioning at this meeting?"

At this stage in the team's maturity, the intervention of the leader at certain points is enough to get the team back on track, for members are now used to handling team actions themselves. However, the role of the team leader is never fixed. Just because he or she has been able to move from educator to coach doesn't mean that there won't be a need for the leader to fill the educator role again. It is quite possible that when new ideas, concepts, or skills are identified, the leader may need to shift back to the educator role or perhaps to the coaching role until the team is comfortable with the new situation.

Leadership Roles in Self-directed Teams

Some organizations create a context for their teams based on the idea that teams need to have more authority to deal with the issues they face. Such teams, often called *self-directed* work teams, are also called *autonomous* or *semiautonomous* work teams. In these types of teams the leader, if one is designated, will typically act in the role of a coach or a facilitator. An autonomous team, however, does not have a formally designated leader. It can select its own leader, rotate leadership among members, or operate without a leader—a kind of "leadership by committee" process during which leadership functions are assigned to different members of the team. A semiautonomous team, by contrast, does have a designated leader with a formal title and position, but the leader's role is defined in such a way that the team makes its own decisions and takes actions independent of the leader. This has led to one of the dilemmas of the semiautonomous team: determining the role of the leader if the team has the right to function without the direct influence and control of that formal leader.

Organizations that have successfully adopted semiautonomous teams have begun to redefine the role of the formal leader in some combination of the following:

- The leader functions primarily as a training resource or facilitator to help the team examine how it is working and give the team the needed training, coaching, or facilitation.
- The leader spends most of his or her time dealing with issues with other units or with upper management. Or the leader may increase the interaction and relationships with customers.

- The leader acts as a consultant to the team and can be asked to help deal with team problems, conflicts, problem members, or other concerns.
- The leader may attend all team meetings or attend only when invited. The leader may formally open the meeting but then turn the activities of the meeting over to team members.

It is apparent that some teams are autonomous or semiautonomous in name only; that is, the formal leader is not willing to relinquish power and continues to function in the traditional leader role of having all activities flow from and through the leader. It should also be apparent that the team can find itself beset with a multitude of problems if team members have never had training or experience in how to work together as a team. Sometimes teams are asked not only to plan, schedule, and coordinate work but also to make decisions about hiring, terminations, allocation of pay raises or bonuses, vacation schedules, training needs, or awarding time off to attend meetings or other activities. These issues, which are central to a number of personal concerns of team members, have proved difficult even for experienced teams, and an untrained autonomous or semiautonomous work team can get buried under a load of activities it is not prepared to handle.

We know of one organization using semiautonomous teams that even made budget cutting and layoff decisions as a team, decisions typically reserved for senior management. When the business experienced a serious downturn, the organization's senior management gave the work teams data on the kinds of budget cuts that were needed to help the business survive, and the teams were then given the autonomy to decide how they would reduce costs, the bulk of which were in payroll. The teams came up with some creative solutions: some team members decided to take unpaid vacations, others decided to job-share or work part time, and still others who wanted to leave the company and had other opportunities were let go. By allowing the team to use its autonomy and creativity in the face of a difficult situation, the company was able to weather the crisis and emerge even stronger.

Identifying Effective Team Leaders

In this chapter we have discussed many of the characteristics of effective team leaders as well as outlined how leadership style needs to change as a team matures and team members are willing and able to accept more responsibility for team performance. Identifying effective team leaders is not an easy task, so we've developed a "Team Leader Survey" which allows an organization's management, team members, and team leaders themselves to determine their strengths and weaknesses as a team leader and hopefully put together a plan for improvement in areas where they are weak.

Team Leader Survey

To what extent does the team leader:	Not at all			To a great extent	
1) Articulate the team's vision and mission	1	2	3	4	5
2) Help the team set clear goals	1	2	3	4	5
3) Articulate the strategy to achieve the vision and goals	1	2	3	4	5
4) Have a good understanding of team's task and what is needed to accomplish it	1	2	3	4	5
5) Help plan and organize the work	1	2	3	4	5
6) Build trust	1	2	3	4	5
7) Follow through on commitments	1	2	3	4	5
8) Provide good feedback to team members	1	2	3	4	5
9) Communicate well	1	2	3	4	5
10) Listen well	1	2	3	4	5

To what extent does the team leader:	Not at all				To a great extent
11) Recognize team members for good performance	1	2	3	4	5
12) Respect others on the team	1	2	3	4	5
13) Delegate effectively	1	2	3	4	5
14) Get resources and support for the team	1	2	3	4	5
15) Treat team members fairly	1	2	3	4	5
16) Show commitment to help the team achieve its goals	1	2	3	4	5
17) Help team members to improve their skills	1	2	3	4	5
18) Motivate members of the team effectively	1	2	3	4	5
19) Encourage innovation and new ideas	1	2	3	4	5
20) Accept responsibility for his/her actions	1	2	3	4	5
21) Inspire the team to perform at a high level	1	2	3	4	5
22) Consult with team members appropriately when a decision needs to be made	1	2	3	4	5
23) Share power appropriately with team members	1	2	3	4	5
24) Lead by setting a good example for team members	1	2	3	4	5

(Continued)

Scoring: Total the points. Team leaders who have a **score from 108 to 120** are generally performing at a high level unless there are some serious problems related to a few of the survey items.

Scores from 96 to 107 would indicate good performance on the part of the team leader.

Scores from 84 from 95 would suggest adequate performance.

A score of 83 or below would indicate relatively poor performance on the part of the team leader.

A score below 70 should call into question the team leader's ability to lead the team unless some significant improvement is made.

What If the Team Leader Is the Problem?

Sometimes the team leader's behavior is the cause of problems in the team. When the leader lacks the skills, insight, and motivation to help the team achieve its goals, conflict is the inevitable result. Sometimes the problem is between the leader and the entire team and sometimes between the leader and one or two members. Either way, unless the leader is aware of the situation and is willing to take steps to remedy the problem, it is difficult for team members to discuss the issue openly with the leader. It is also not uncommon for leaders to be totally or partially unaware of the problems they are causing. In power relationships subordinates have learned to become quite skilled at masking negative feelings and pretending everything is going well.

When symptoms of major problems in the team emerge, the team leader should ask, "Is it possible that I am at least partly responsible for these problems?" How does a team leader get an honest answer to this question?

1. *Ask the team members.* Either in a team meeting or in an interview one-on-one with the team members, the team leader might say something like this: "I want you to level with me.

I know that things have not been going well in our team (describe some of the symptoms). I want to know if I am responsible for creating negative reactions in the group. I would appreciate it if you could let me know, either openly now or in an email or memo later, what things I am doing that create problems and any suggestions you have that would improve matters." In asking for feedback, it is often useful if the leader can identify some things he or she has done that may have caused problems for the team member. For example, the leader might say to the team member: "I think that I sometimes come to meetings with my mind already made up and then put pressure on people to agree with me; do you see this behavior in me? (Wait for the response.) If you do, what suggestions do you have that will help me avoid this kind of problem?" If there is a lack of trust in the group or in certain team members, this direct approach may not work. This means that the leader may then need to resort to other means of getting feedback.

2. *Use an outside resource*. A common method of getting information to the leader is to find an outside person, either outside the team but in the organization (a human resource specialist) or an external consultant. A skilled outside resource can interview team members and try to elicit data about the involvement of the team leader in team problems. This information can then be fed back to the leader and a strategy devised for using the information with the team.

3. *Use instruments*. Currently many survey instruments are available for gathering data, anonymously if necessary, from subordinates about their perceptions of the leader. These data would need to be gathered and analyzed by someone other than the team leader to ensure anonymity. A human resource person is useful for handling this task and then seeing that the data are summarized and returned to the team leader. Then a method for using this information with the team needs to be devised. One method is for the manager to present a summary of data to the group, indicate acceptance of the data, announce some

preliminary actions that will be taken, and ask the team members to suggest other appropriate changes.

4. *Undertake training.* Another approach is to have the team leader go to a training program that features giving feedback to all participants on their interpersonal style. The team leader then brings a summary of this feedback to the team, checks with them about its validity, and works out a program of improvement.

If team leaders want to get feedback on their performance, there are several options; a more difficult issue remains if the leader is unaware of his or her impact or does not seem to want to find out. In such a situation there are a few options for team members.

1. *Suggest a role-clarification session.* Such a session could allow the team members to identify actions they need from the team leader or changes they feel would improve activities in the team. This exercise is described in detail in Chapter 8.

2. *Give direct feedback.* Obviously one possibility is for team members to find an opportunity to give direct, albeit unsolicited, feedback to the leader. Despite the inherent risks, the team—either altogether or through representatives—could say to the leader, "We have a dilemma. There are problems in the team that we feel involve you. Our dilemma is we think we should share this information with you, but we do not want to disrupt our relationship with you. Do you have any suggestions as to how we might deal with this dilemma?" This approach usually results in the leader's asking for the data in a far different atmosphere than confronting the leader unexpectedly with difficult feedback.

3. *Use an outside facilitator.* It is also possible for the team to go to an appropriate internal resource person (typically from human resources) and ask for assistance. Often the outside person can then go to the leader and suggest a set of alternatives that might surface the concerns of the team.

Notes

1. L. C. McDermott, N. Brawley, and W. W. Waite, *World Class Teams: Working Across Borders* (New York: Wiley, 1998).
2. The Peter Principle is articulated by Laurence Peter in which he suggests that managers are promoted to their level of incompetence—thus they reach a ceiling where they aren't promotable. Thus Peter argues that many leaders have risen to their level of incompetence.

7

DESIGNING EFFECTIVE
TEAM-BUILDING PROGRAMS

Now that we have examined each of the 5Cs and described how they can be applied to improve team performance, we'll focus on how organizations can become "team-oriented" by applying the 5C model. In this chapter we discuss how organizations can put together team development programs to improve the performance of their teams. The goal of any organization-wide team development program is to help the teams in the organization engage in a continual process of self-examination to gain awareness of those conditions—context, composition, competencies, change management, and collaborative leadership—that keep them from functioning effectively.

In Chapter 5, we identified a number of symptoms of unhealthy teams. Having gathered data about such problems, teams must learn how to use the data to make decisions and take actions that will change the team context, composition, competencies, change management or leadership in ways that will lead to better performance. As mentioned previously, team-oriented organizations see effective teamwork as a key organizational success factor. Thus, orchestrating the development of effective teams is viewed as an ongoing process, not a one-time activity.

As we noted in Chapter 5, a team development generally begins with a block of time, usually two or three days, during which the team learns how to engage in its own review, analysis, action planning, and decision making, then starts taking action.

Following the first team meetings, the team may periodically take other blocks of time to continue the process, review progress made since the last team meeting, and identify what should be done to continue to improve the team's overall effectiveness. It is also possible that in time the team will develop its skills for development to such a point that team members are always aware of areas that need improvement and will raise them at appropriate times with the appropriate people, thereby making it unnecessary to set aside a special meeting for such action.

We have found that it is essential for top management to commit to creating the right context for team development by providing teams with the time and resources. Too many times we have seen team development initiatives undermined and fail because senior managers were not willing to give a team the time and resources needed to examine how it has been functioning and take steps to improve performance.

There is no single way to put together a program of team improvement. The format depends on the experience, interests, and needs of the team members; the experience and needs of the team leader; the skills of the consultant (if one is needed); the nature of the situation that has prompted the need for team building; and the expectations of the organization in regard to team development. Some organizations regularly survey team members and provide feedback on each team's performance to ensure that teams will engage in self-reflection and take action to improve the team.

This chapter describes a range of design alternatives for each phase of a team-building program. Organization leaders may wish to select various design elements from among the alternatives that seem applicable to their own organizations and their specific situation. Although the design of a team-building program generally follows the cycle described in Chapter 5, in this chapter we outline some of the specific steps and actions that we take when designing a program.

Phase 1: Preparation for Team Building

There are certain phases or steps in any team-building program. The first phase concerns describing the purpose of the program and introducing the program to team members. We will briefly describe the options available for team leaders as they begin to prepare their teams for team building.

Goals

The goals of this initial phase are to explain the purpose of team building, elicit agreement to work on certain problems, get commitment for participation, and do preliminary work for the team-building workshop. Any team-building program must be well conceived, and those involved must have indicated at least a minimal commitment to participate. Commitment will increase if people understand clearly why the program is being proposed and if they can participate in creating the program.

If this is the first time the team has spent some time together with the specific assignment to review their effectiveness and plan for change, they will likely be anxious and apprehensive. These concerns must be brought to the surface and addressed. Questions of deep concern probably will not be eliminated. However, team members' concerns may be reduced as a supportive climate is established and as people test the water and find that plunging in is not very difficult. Experience will be the best teacher, and people will allay or confirm their fears as the session proceeds. Those conducting the session should anticipate such concerns and raise them prior to the first meeting to reduce any extreme anxiety by openly describing what will happen and what the anticipated outcome will be.

Alternative Actions

Among the possible actions that managers might take to get started are these:

1. Have an outside person, possibly from human resources, interview each team member to identify problems, concerns, and the need for change.

2. Invite an expert on teams to talk about the role of teams in organizations and the purposes of team development. The speaker might discuss the Five Cs of team performance and how they relate to the performance of that team.

3. Gather data on the level of team effectiveness. (See the team-building checklist at the end of Chapter 5 and the other surveys presented in this book or online.)

4. Have a general discussion about the need for developing team competencies.

5. Invite a manager who has had successful team-building experiences to describe the activities and results in his or her team.

After this initial preparation phase, team members should: (1) understand the need for team development; (2) have their fears and concerns addressed regarding a team-building program; and (3) have a general understanding of the process to be followed in developing the team. Also, if team members see that such a process is an *organization-wide* effort to improve all the teams in the organization and that they are not being singled out, they will be more likely to accept and be committed to a team-building program. Moreover, such an organization-wide effort allows idea sharing between teams regarding their team-building efforts, which can create an atmosphere conducive to improving teams across the organization.

Phase 2: Create an Open Climate and Gather Data

The second phase of the team-building program is to create a climate for gathering and sharing data. The goals for this phase and alternative approaches are as follows:

Goals

The goals of this phase are to create a climate for team members to focus on team issues; establish norms for being open with problems, concerns, and ideas for planning and for dealing with issues; and, present a framework for the whole experience. The climate established during the start-up phase influences the rest of the program.

Once a climate of openness and sharing has been developed, team members are more likely to generate good data regarding the team. In some cases, the organization may have already developed a common methodology for gathering data about its teams (e.g. Bain). However, in most instances, given that each team may be in a different situation, the team should be able to choose what data gathering approach would make the most sense for itself. If the team has input regarding how and what type of data should be gathered, the data are generally seen as more valid and acceptable to team members.

Alternative I

One way to begin this process is to have the team leader give a short opening talk, reviewing the goals for the team as he or she sees them, and the need for the program, emphasizing his or her support, and reaffirming the norm that no negative sanctions are intended for any open, honest behavior. The role of the consultant, if there is one, can be explained by either the manager or the consultant.

Participants can share their immediate here-and-now feelings about the meetings by responding to questions handed out on a sheet of paper, like the ones shown in the "Attitudes about Change" worksheet. They call out their answers (to set the norm of open sharing of data), and the person at the flipchart records the responses.

Attitudes About Change

Instructions: Answer the following questions on a scale of 1 to 5.

1. How confident are you that any real change will result from these meetings?

1	2	3	4	5
I am not confident at all.		I am somewhat confident.		I am highly confident.

2. To what degree do you feel that people really want to be here and work on team development issues?

1	2	3	4	5
People don't really want to be here.		People have some interest in being here.		People have high interest in being here.

3. How willing do you think people are to make changes that may be suggested?

1	2	3	4	5
People will be unwilling to change.		People have some willingness to change.		People are very willing to change.

---

4. How willing do you think you and others will be to express real
    feelings and concerns?

1	2	3	4	5
We are not very willing to express feelings.		We have some degree of willingness to express feelings.		We are very willing to express feelings.

The results are tallied (with high and low scores on each item
and the mean score) and presented to the team. After seeing the
results, the team should be asked to discuss these questions: Why
are the scores rather low (or high)? What could be done here to
help people feel more positive about team development? If the team
is large, subgroups should be created to discuss these questions for
20 minutes and report back to the entire team.

This exercise sets the norm that the program is centered on data
gathering, data analysis, open sharing, and trying to plan based on
good data. This also allows group members to test the water about
simple, immediate data, rather than more sensitive team issues, and
for the leader to see how they will respond and react to the questions.

Alternative 2

After preliminary remarks by the manager, the team members could
be asked, "For us to get a picture of how you see our team functioning,
please take a few minutes to describe our team as a kind of animal
or combination of animals, a kind of machine, a kind of person, or

whatever image comes to mind." Some teams in the past have been described as:

- A hunting dog—a pointer: "We run around and locate problems, then stop and point and hope that somebody else will take the action."
- A Cadillac with bicycle pedals: "We look good on the outside, but there is no real power to get us moving."
- A centipede with several missing or broken legs: "Although the centipede can move forward, its progress is crippled by the missing and broken legs."
- An octopus: "Each tentacle is out grasping anything it can but doesn't know what the other tentacles are doing."

As people share the images and explain why they came to mind, some questions for follow-up are: What are the common elements in these images? Do we like these images of ourselves? What do we need to do to change our image? Discussion aimed at answering these questions becomes the major agenda item for subsequent meetings.

Alternative 3

In this scenario, under the guidance of a consultant or facilitator, the team works on a major decision-making problem—such as an arctic or desert survival exercise—and to function under the direction of the team leader in a fashion similar to the way they have previously worked on problems.[1] The facilitator acts as a process observer for the exercise. In most instances it helps to have the team videotaped as it does the exercise so it can be reviewed afterward. After the exercise, the consultant has the group members watch the videotape and review their decision-making processes to determine both their strengths and their deficiencies in solving problems. The facilitator shares his or her observations with the group.

As the exercise is reviewed, lists of positive and negative features are compiled. The agenda for the following session is set, based on the question, "How do we maximize our strengths and overcome deficiencies?" For example, if the process review indicates that the group is highly dependent on the leader, that some people are overwhelmed by the "big talker," or that the group jumps to decisions before everyone has a chance to put in ideas, the agenda would focus on how to reduce or change these negative conditions.

Alternative 4

This alternative starts with the team leader describing the 5Cs of team performance to members of the team. With the 5Cs listed on a whiteboard or flipchart, the team then discusses each of the 5Cs in turn, listing those attributes of each C that either help their team perform better or hinder the team's performance. The end result of this exercise is a list of the 5Cs with those factors that "help" or "hinder" team performance. Or in similar fashion the team leader can facilitate a discussion on what the team should "start" and "stop" or "continue" doing within each C in order to improve team functioning. For teams that want to gather additional data on each of the 5Cs, they might want team members to fill out the surveys on the 5Cs found in this book, summarize the results, and then use that data to begin to problem-solve.

Phase 3: Group Data Analysis and Problem Solving

After the team has understood the purpose of the team-building program and data has been generated regarding the team's functioning and performance, the next phase is to focus on analyzing the data and develop a plan of action to solve the team's problems.

Goals

One goal of this phase is to develop plans to solve the problems identified in the previous phase. Another goal is for the team to practice better problem-solving, decision-making, planning, and delegation skills. Whatever the start-up method or combination of methods used, this third phase usually has two parts: (1) the team begins to engage in the problem-solving process, and (2) a process consultant or observer helps the group look at its context, composition, competencies, change management, and leadership in working on problems as an effective team as a prelude to improving its problem-solving capabilities.

In examining the data, the team typically discovers several problems hindering the team's performance. Ineffective teams are often characterized by one or more of the following conditions:

- Domination by the leader
- Warring cliques or subgroups
- Unequal participation and uneven use of group resources
- Rigid or dysfunctional group norms and procedures
- A climate of defensiveness or fear
- A lack of creative alternatives to problems
- Restricted communications—not all having opportunities to speak
- Avoidance of differences or potential conflicts
- People not feeling rewarded for good performance

Such conditions reduce the team's ability to work together in collective problem-solving situations. The role of the team leader or consultant is to help the group become aware of its processes and begin to develop better team competencies. Specifically, after becoming aware of a process problem (e.g. the leader dominates the conversation) the team needs to establish a procedure, guideline, or plan of action to respond to the negative condition.

Alternatives for Analyzing the Data

There are several alternatives to analyze the data that have been gathered and generate solutions. These are as follows:

Alternative 1 Following the opening remarks, the consultant, outside person, or team leader presents data that have been collected prior to the meeting. The team is then asked to analyze the data. What do the data mean? Why do we respond the way we do? What conditions give rise to negative responses? What do we need to change to get a more positive response to our own team? The team might sort the data into the categories of context, composition, competencies, change, and collaborative leadership to identify the root causes of the team's problems. In larger teams this analysis is best be done in subgroups of three to four people and then shared with the whole group and compiled into a list of issues and possible change actions.

Alternative 2 This design requires some extensive case analysis prior to the team-building sessions. The team leader or consultant writes up vignettes, or critical incidents that seem to represent recurring problems for the team. Another possibility is to have each member take a problem area for him or her and write it up as a short case. The group task is to look at the cases, try to discern the underlying conditions that trigger recurring problems, and then plan action steps for reducing the likelihood that such problems will reoccur.

Alternative 3 In this alternative, objective data gathered from records about the team are compiled and presented to the group members. Such information as sales, production records, the grievance rate, absenteeism, turnover, lost time, budget discrepancies, late reports, cost increases, and so on are included in this feedback. The team's job is to conduct an in-depth analysis of the data, diagnose the causes of any negative trends, and then plan for improvement.

Alternative 4 Instead of presenting to the team data from prior data collection methods, data about the conditions or problems of the team can be raised at the team meeting. Each person is asked to come prepared to share his or her answers to the following questions:

• What keeps this team from functioning at its maximum potential?

- What keeps you personally from doing the kind of job you would like to do?
- What things do you like in this team that you want to have maintained?
- What changes would you like to see made that would help you and the whole team?

Team members or the leader may have other items they would like to put on the agenda. Each team member takes a turn sharing information. The responses are listed and common themes identified. The most important issues are listed in priority, and they become the items for discussion.

The Problem-Solving Process

At this point, regardless of the alternative selected, the team should have identified a series of problems, concerns, or issues. If the team leader or facilitator hasn't shared the 5C model already, it can be helpful to share the model and then sort the problems the team faces into the five categories: context problems, composition problems, competency problems, change management problems, and leadership problems. In this way, the team can determine which problems reside within the team and which are related to issues that may not be under the team's direct control.

The team can then move into a traditional problem-solving process by engaging in the following actions:

1. Put problems in order of priority and select the most pressing ones to address.
2. Begin the classic problem-solving process: clearly define the problem, describe the causes of the problem, list alternative solutions, select the alternative to implement, develop an action plan, perform the action, and evaluate the results.
3. Set up task force teams or subunits. Give each team a problem to work on. It should develop a plan of action, carry out the plan, and assess the results.

4. After all problems have been listed, the team can sort them into the categories we described in Chapter 5: (A) problems are ones that we can work here within our team, (B) problems are those that someone else must handle (identify who that person - or persons - is and develop a strategy to influence that person), or (C) problems are ones that we must learn to live with since it appears to be beyond our ability to change; thus, we need to develop a coping strategy to deal with this condition.

5. Set targets, objectives, or goals. The team should spend time identifying short- or long-range goals it wishes to achieve, make assignments, and set target dates for completion.

Using Feedback to Improve Team Performance

A major issue that often arises following the identification of problems is the sharing of feedback with individuals, subgroups within the team, or the team as a whole. Certain actions, functions, personal styles, or strategies on the part of one or more people may be hindering teamwork and preventing other team members from achieving their goals or feeling satisfied with the team. If this is the case, it may be legitimate to engage in an open feedback session.

Goals

The team should share feedback among individual team members in such a way as to help them improve their effectiveness and give feedback to the whole team with the same objective in mind. The goal of a feedback session is to share data about performance so that difficulties can be resolved. It is critical that a feedback session not slip into name calling, personal griping, or verbal punishing of others. All feedback should reflect a genuine willingness to work cooperatively. For example, one might say, "My performance suffers because of some things that happen in which you are involved. Let me share my feelings and reactions so you can see what is happening to me. I would like to come up with a way that we all can work more productively together."

Types of Feedback

Feedback is most helpful if it can be given in descriptive fashion or in the form of suggestions. The team leader or consultant should review with the team the differences between "descriptive" and "evaluative" feedback and be willing to "correct" team members if they give inappropriate feedback. Here are some examples of ways to give feedback that reduce defensiveness.

- *Descriptive feedback:* "John, when you promise me that you will have a report ready at a certain time, as happened last Thursday, and I don't get it, that really frustrates me. It puts me behind schedule and makes me feel very resentful toward you. Are you aware that such things are going on? Do you know what is causing the problem or have any ideas on how we could avoid this type of problem in the future?"

- *Suggestions:* "John, let me make a suggestion that would really help me as we work together. If you could get your reports to me on time, particularly those that have been promised at a certain time, it would help my work schedule and reduce my frustration. Also, if I don't get a report on time, what would you prefer I do about it?"

- *Other possibilities:* The following are some other ways group members might go about sharing feedback with one another:
  - *Stop-start-continue activity.* Each person has a sheet of paper on the wall. Each team member writes on the sheets of other members items in three areas: things that person should begin doing that will increase his or her effectiveness, things the individual should stop doing, and things he or she should continue to do.
  - *Envelope exchange.* Each person writes a note to other team members with specific, individual feedback, covering the same issues as in the previous activity, and gives the notes to the other team members. This can be done anonymously, but

team members must be coached on how to respond to critical feedback. In most cases, however, the person giving the feedback should attach his or her name to it so the person receiving the feedback can understand where it is coming from. That way they can jointly engage in discussions to address the feedback.

o *Confirmation–disconfirmation process*. Group members summarize how they view themselves and their own work performance—their strengths and areas that need improvement. Others are asked to confirm or disconfirm the person's diagnosis.

o *Management profile*. Each person presents the profile of his or her effectiveness from previously gathered data (there are a variety of profile instruments). The group confirms or disconfirms the profile.

o *Analysis of subunits*. If the team has subunits, each subunit is discussed in terms of what it does well, what it needs to change, and what it needs to improve.

o *Total unit or organizational analysis*. The entire team, department, division, or organization looks at how it has been functioning and critiques its own performance over the past year, identifying things it has done well and areas that need improvement. Group size is, of course, the main constraint with this option. Beckhard and Weisbord have developed approaches for working with large groups, and we recommend reading their works before conducting this type of activity.[2]

o *Open feedback session*. Each person who would like feedback may ask for it in order to identify areas of personal effectiveness and areas that need improvement.

o *Prescription writing*. Each person writes a prescription for others: "Here is what I would prescribe that you do [or stop doing] in order to be more effective in your position." Prescriptions are then exchanged.

Phase 4: Action Planning

The end result of all the activities mentioned so far is to help the team identify conditions that are blocking both individual and team effectiveness so that the team can begin to develop plans for action and change. Action plans should include a commitment to carry the action to completion as well as metrics to determine whether the goal has been achieved.

Goals

The goals of this phase are to pinpoint needed changes, set goals, develop plans, give assignments, outline procedures, and set dates for completion and review. Often the plan is a set of agreements on who is willing to take a specific action. All such agreements should be written down, circulated, and followed up later to ensure that they have been carried out.

Options for Action Planning

Following is a set of actions that are possible during this phase:

1. *Personal improvement plan.* Each person evaluates his or her feedback and develops a plan of action for personal improvement. This plan is presented to the others.
2. *Contract negotiations.* If there are particular problems between individuals or subunits, specific agreements for dealing with conflict issues are drawn up and signed.
3. *Assignment summary.* Each person summarizes what his or her assignments are and the actions he or she intends to take as a follow-up to what has been agreed upon.
4. *Subunit or team plans.* If development plans have been completed, they are presented and reviewed.
5. *Schedule review.* The team looks at its time schedule and its action plans. Dates for completion and dates for giving progress

reports on work being done are confirmed. The next team meeting is scheduled. If another team development workshop or meeting is needed, it may be scheduled at this time.

Phase 5: Implementation, Evaluation, and Follow-Up

Follow-up is an integral part of any team-building program. There must be some method of following up with team members on assignments or agreements, and then some form of continuing goal setting for improved performance. These follow-up activities can be done by the whole team together, one-on-one between team members and the team leader, or a combination of the two. Fortunately, some excellent research has been done that describes follow-up processes that have proved to be successful.

Wayne Boss of the University of Colorado became interested in the "regression effect" following a team-building session.[3] He observed, as have others, that during a two- or three-day intensive team-building activity, people become very enthusiastic about making improvements, but within a few weeks, the spark dwindles, and they regress to old behaviors and performance levels. Boss wondered whether there is a way to keep performance high following the team-building session and to prevent regression. He began to experiment with a one-on-one follow-up meeting he called the personal management interview (PMI).

The PMI has two stages. First is a role negotiation meeting between team leader and subordinate (usually lasting one hour) during which both clarify their expectations of each other, what they need from each other, and what they will contract to do for each other. Second, following the initial role negotiation session, the two parties meet regularly. Boss found that these meetings have to be held on a regular basis (weekly, biweekly, or monthly), but if they are held and follow the agreed-on agenda, performance stays high without regression for several years. Boss states that, "Without exception, the off-site level of group effectiveness was maintained only in those teams that employed the PMI, while the teams that did not use the PMI evidenced substantial regression in the months after their team-building session."[4]

What goes on in these interviews that makes such a difference? Despite some variation, each interview tended to deal with the following issues:

- Discussion of any organizational or work problems facing the subordinate
- Training or coaching given by the team leader to the subordinate
- Resolution of any concerns or problems between the team leader and subordinate
- Information sharing to bring the subordinate up to date on what is happening in the team and organization
- Discussion of any personal problems or concerns

These were common agenda items, but the first part of every meeting was spent reviewing assignments and accomplishments since the previous session. Time was also spent on making new assignments, and agreeing on goals and plans to review at the next PMI. These assignments and agreements were written down, and both parties had a copy that was the basis of the review at the following meeting.

Boss has the following suggestions for conducting an effective PMI:

- The PMI is most effective when conducted in a climate of high support and trust. Establishing this climate is primarily the responsibility of the superior.
- The interviews must be held on a regular basis and be free from interruptions.
- Both parties must prepare for the meeting by having an agreed-on agenda; otherwise, the PMI becomes nothing more than conversation without clear goals.
- When possible, a third party whom both the team leader and the subordinate trust should be present to take notes and record action items.

- Meetings should be documented by use of a standard form to make sure the key issues are addressed in a systematic way. Both parties agree on the form.
- The leader must be willing to hold subordinates accountable and ask the difficult *why* questions when assignments are not completed.

Boss has found that performance drops off if these meetings are not held but increases if meetings are started, even if they have never been held before or had been stopped for a time. Boss has tracked the use of PMIs in 202 teams across time periods ranging from three months to 29 years.[5] His research indicates that regular PMIs (at least monthly) can significantly decrease, and even prevent, regression to previous levels of team performance for as long as 29 years with no additional interventions after the original team-building sessions. Certainly the evidence is compelling enough to indicate that this is an effective way to follow up on decisions made during a team-building session.

Boss's research does not discuss any further team sessions. Some teams that have used the PMI have also reported having regular team meetings to deal with issues common to all, as well as additional team development sessions every three to six months. These later sessions identify any current problems or concerns and establish new goals for change and plans for improvement. As noted previously, Bain & Company does monthly reviews of team performance.

In the past, many teams have followed up a team-building session with additional team meetings to review progress. The advantage of the PMI is that it allows time to talk with each person individually. If this were done in the presence of the whole team, it could be both inhibiting and extremely time-consuming.

Follow-Up Team Sessions

We have known for many years, since the early research of Rensis Likert, that follow-up team sessions can also help to sustain high performance.[6] In his research on sales teams, Likert described the elements of follow-up team meetings that make a significant difference in the performance of members on the team. The top 20 sales units were compared with the bottom 20 to see what made the difference in their performance. Likert found the following to be the most important factors:

- The team leader (the sales manager) had high personal performance goals and a plan for achieving those goals. Team members saw an example of high performance as they watched the team leader.

- The team leader displayed highly supportive behavior toward team members and encouraged them to support one another.

- The team leader used participative methods in supervision. That is, all team members were involved in helping the team and the members achieve their goals.

The major process for achieving high performance was holding regular, well-planned meetings of the sales team for review of each person's performance. In contrast to Boss's PMI, a one-on-one follow-up interview, the units in the Likert research used team meetings as the follow-up process. Those team meetings had the following major features:

- The team met regularly every two weeks or every month.

- The size of the team varied but was usually between 12 and 15 members.

- The sales manager presided over the meeting but allowed wide participation in the group. The main function of the manager was to keep the team focused on the task; encourage the team to set high performance goals; and discourage negative, ego-deflating actions of team members.

- Each salesperson presented a report of his or her activities during the previous period, including a description of the approach used, closings attempted, sales achieved, and volume and quality of total sales.

- All of the other team members analyzed the person's efforts and offered suggestions for improvement. Coaching was given by team members to one another. This process encouraged team members to learn from each other.
- Each salesperson announced his or her goals and procedures to be used, which would be reviewed at the next team meeting.

The researchers concluded that this form of team meeting results in four benefits:

1. Team members set higher goals.
2. They are more motivated to achieve their goals.
3. They receive more assistance, coaching, and help from their leader and peers.
4. The team gets more new ideas on how to improve performance as people share, instead of keeping secret, their successful new methods.

It seems possible, then, to have either one-on-one follow-up meetings or a series of follow-up team meetings as a way of maintaining the high performance of team members. The key issue is that team building requires a continuous effort to monitor the team's ability to improve team performance. The key person is the team leader, who must build a follow-up procedure into the process.

While the two most common follow-up methods are one-on-one interviews and follow-up team meetings, other follow-up procedures are available, depending on the nature of the team's problems and plans. For example, a follow-up data-gathering process can use a survey or questionnaire to see if the unit members feel the activities of the team have improved. Another approach is to have an outsider interview members to check on what has improved and what actions are still needed. Alternatively, an outside observer could be invited to watch the team in action and give a process review at the end of the meeting.

If a team has poor interaction at meetings, it is possible to follow up with a procedure to get reactions of people after each meeting or after some meetings. The team leaders could use a short paper-and-pencil survey or ask for a critique of the meeting verbally, posing questions such as the following:

- How satisfied were you with the team meeting today?
- Are there any actions we keep doing that restrict our effectiveness?
- What do we need to stop doing, start doing, or continue doing that would improve our team performance?
- Do we really function as a team, or are there indications that teamwork is lacking?
- Are we achieving our goals and using each person's resources effectively?

If your team discusses these questions, be sure to allot sufficient time for an adequate critique. If you use a written form, summarize the results and begin the next team meeting by reviewing the summary and discussing what should be done in the current meeting to make the team more effective.

Notes

1. For a description of a variety of team-building activities, see www .pfeiffer.com and review the books and exercises developed by Lorraine L. Ukens or Steve Sugar and George Takac (*Games That Team Teams: 21 Activities to Super-Charge Your Group!*) or see B. C. Miller's *Quick Teambuilding Activities for Busy Managers: 50 Exercises That Get Results in Just 15 Minutes* (New York: Amacom, 2004).
2. R. Beckhard, "The Confrontation Meeting," *Harvard Business Review* 45 (1967): 149–55; M. Weisboard and S. Janoff, *Future Search: Getting the Whole System in the Room for Vision, Commitment, and Action* (San Francisco: Berrett-Koehler, 2010).
3. R. W. Boss, *Organization Development in Health Care, Part II* (Reading, MA: Addison-Wesley, 1989).

4. R. W. Boss, "Team Building and the Problem of Regression: The Personal Management Interview as an Intervention," *Journal of Applied Behavioral Science* 19 (1983): 75.

5. R. W. Boss, personal communication.

6. R. Likert, *The Human Organization* (New York: McGraw-Hill, 1967), chap. 4.

8

SPECIFIC TEAM-BUILDING INTERVENTIONS TO ADDRESS TEAM PROBLEMS

In Chapter 7 we described the characteristics of effective team-building programs. In this chapter, we will turn our attention to specific team interventions that we have found to be particularly helpful in improving team performance. These interventions are: (1) stop-start-continue activity; (2) force field analysis; (3) role clarification; and (4) appreciative inquiry. In addition to internal team conflict, we have found that there is often conflict *between* teams. Thus, we've also included interventions that we have used to manage inter-team conflict.

The Start-Stop-Continue Exercise

If the team is having performance problems and needs to quickly develop plans for improvement, we recommend the start-stop-continue exercise since it's relatively easy to understand and carry out. In this team-building exercise, each person lists what the team as a whole needs to (1) start doing, (2) stop doing, and (3) continue doing in order to improve performance. This process gives each team member the opportunity to clarify how the team should change—but also what current team activities or processes it should continue. Starting at the team level is a way to eventually examine the individual behaviors of team members. This process typically identifies areas where team members are in conflict in terms of expectations and priorities. So the team leader needs to be prepared to manage those conflicts as they arise. Each person explains to the team, or lists on the whiteboard, the things he or

135

she would like to see the team or certain team members start doing, stop doing, and continue doing if expectations are to be met and positive results achieved.

With the lists of things that each party wants from the other on display for all to see, a discussion ensues. The first step is to identify areas of agreement with regard to what the team should start, stop, and continue doing.

The second step is to identify areas of difference. During this second step it may be helpful to facilitate a negotiation among team members to reach a compromise or ensure that team members get at least something that is important to them. For example, subgroup A (or person A) may agree on what it will do in return for a similar behavioral change on the part of subgroup B (or person B). Such agreements should be written up because a written agreement usually increases commitment to making the change and helps to avoid any misunderstandings (in some cases to ensure commitment it might make sense to have all team members sign the agreement to signal their commitment). This process puts the formerly disputing factions into a problem-solving situation that requires them to try to work out solutions rather than spend time finding fault or placing blame.

The design of this type of meeting can vary widely. It may be desirable to precede the session with a presentation of the 5C model and discussion of those factors that can hinder team performance, thus getting team members to think more broadly about what might be affecting the team. Another possibility is to have each team member try to predict what the other team members think about them and what they think the other members want from them. These guesses are often surprisingly accurate and may help in reaching an agreement and common mutual expectations.

A similar design may also be used to negotiate agreements between individuals. If there are disagreements among team members at any point, it is often best to stop and work out a negotiation, coming to an agreement with other team members present. However, be aware if the negotiation is likely to take an inordinate amount of time which could cause other team members who aren't involved in the conflict to lose interest in the process. Under such circumstances, the team leader can meet with the parties in conflict at a later date to hammer out an agreement that is then shared with the rest of the team.

Negotiation often involves compromise: each party gives up something to receive something of similar value from the other. Too frequently, however, conflicts are handled inappropriately by people engaging in the following activities:

- *Ignoring*—trying to pretend that no disagreement exists.
- *Smoothing*—trying to placate people and attempting to get them to feel good even though an agreement has not been reached.
- *Forcing*—getting agreement from a position of power. If the more powerful person forces the other to agree, the result may be public agreement but private resistance.

When an effective team experiences conflict, the team should take time to identify the cause of it. The team identifies the conflict as a problem to be solved and takes problem-solving actions. The facilitator (usually team leader) must be perceptive enough to ensure that ignoring, smoothing, or forcing behaviors must not occur during the team-building session. Otherwise the problems will not be resolved and conflict will quickly reemerge.

Force Field Analysis

Another useful intervention is what Kurt Lewin called "force field analysis." Lewin saw social systems much like forces in nature where some forces are moving things in a certain direction while other forces are pushing in the opposite direction. Under such conditions a state of "equilibrium" between the various forces would eventually be reached. In the case of a team, certain forces (behaviors, processes, practices, attitudes, resources) positively "drive" the performance of the team while other forces "restrain" the team's effectiveness, thus leading to an equilibrium of performance between the driving and restraining forces.

This exercise works well when the team needs to focus on one performance measure at a time. To begin the exercise, the team leader draws a straight, horizontal line on a whiteboard or flipchart which represents the current level of performance on dimension of interest (e.g. revenue growth, productivity, absenteeism) and asks the team: "What is our performance level?" In many cases, the performance measure will be objective (e.g. revenue growth), which will be rather easy to discern from records, but in other cases (e.g. morale) the level of performance will require some discussion among team members until they reach consensus.

Once the team's baseline of performance is determined and listed next to the horizontal line, the team leader then asks: "What forces are pushing our performance down to its current level?" The team then identifies the "restraining forces" that are undermining performance. Arrows, with differing strengths indicating the significance of the restraining force, are then put above the horizontal line pointing down toward it and labeled. After doing this, the team leader asks: "What forces are driving our performance forward to its currently level?" The team then places arrows of differing lengths below the horizontal line of performance which identify those positive forces that are encouraging high performance. Once this exercise is completed, the team will have a "force field model" like that presented in Figure 8.1.

Figure 8.1 Force Field Analysis

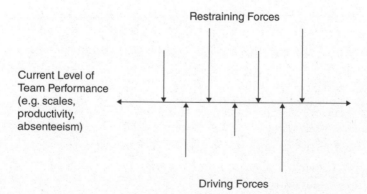

After putting the force-field model together, the team begins problem-solving to improve the performance of the team along the horizontal line. There are basically two ways to do this. Eliminate or reduce some of the restraining forces that are pushing down on the performance line from above, or add to and strengthen the driving forces pushing up from below. The team then identifies specific actions that are needed to raise the performance line. It is important to note that Lewin's research suggested that addressing and eliminating the retraining forces is a more successful way to improve performance on a particular dimension than focusing on increasing the driving forces. Lewin conjectures that performance more easily and naturally improves by removing the roadblocks. One nice thing about this intervention is that the team can visualize the dynamics in play that are affecting the performance of the team, and helps the team focus on the specific forces that are driving and restraining performance.

Helping Teams in Conflict or Confusion: The Role-Clarification Exercise

A particularly useful intervention for clarifying expectations that team members have for one another is what we call the "role-clarification exercise." A role-clarification intervention is considered appropriate if one or more of the following conditions are present:

- The team is newly organized, and no one has a clear understanding about what others do and what others expect of them.
- Changes and reassignments have been made in the team, and there is a lack of clarity about how the various functions and positions now fit together.
- Job descriptions are old and not consistent with current realities.
- Meetings are held infrequently and only for passing on needed directions.

- People carry out their assignments with very little contact with others in the same office. They generally feel isolated.

- Conflicts and interpersonal disruptions in the team seem to be increasing. Coffee-break talk and other informal communications center on discussion of overlaps and encroachments by others on work assignments. People get requests they don't understand. They hear through the grapevine about what others are doing; it sounds as if it's something they should know about, but nobody informs them.

- The team leader engages primarily in one-on-one management. Team meetings are infrequent or primarily involve listening to the leader raise issues with one individual at a time while others watch and wait for their turn. Almost no problem solving is done as a team or between people.

- People sit in their offices and wonder, "What is happening on this team? I don't know what others are doing, and I'm sure nobody knows [or cares] what I'm doing."

- A crisis occurs because everyone thought someone else was responsible for handling a task that was never completed.

Planning

The following describes the steps of a role-clarification exercise. Over the years, we have found this to be one of the most useful exercises for a team to engage in with generally very positive results. However, the facilitator for this exercise must plan carefully to have the time and commitments necessary to perform the intervention.

Time Commitment For a team of eight to ten people, the minimum time needed for this type of team building is approximately one-half to one hour for each person, or a total of four to ten hours of meeting time, preferably in a solid block. With a training day from 8:30 a.m. to 12:00 p.m. and 1:00 to 4:30 p.m., this typically could be achieved in one day. It also would be possible to conduct this type of team-building session by taking one afternoon a week over a period of time. Our experience, however, indicates that spending the time in one block has more impact. Each time a group meets, a certain amount of settling-in time is required, which is minimized if only one session is held.

Resource Personnel If the ground rules, procedures, overall goals, and design elements are clear, the team leader need not be afraid to conduct this type of meeting with no outside assistance from a consultant or facilitator. If certain concerns suggest that an outside person would be helpful in facilitating the meeting, one could be included. This person may be someone from within the organization but in a different department, such as a human resource or organization development specialist, or a consultant from the outside. Regardless of whether an outside resource person is used, the entire team-building meeting should be conducted and managed by the team leader. Team building is management's business; it is the leader building his or her team, not something that should be outsourced to a person in human resources.

Program Design Goal The goal of a role clarification is to arrive at that condition in which all members of the team can publicly agree that they:

- Have a clear understanding of the major requirements of their own job.
- Feel that the others at the meeting also clearly understand everyone's position and duties.
- Know what others expect of them in their working relationships.
- Feel that all know what others need from them in their working relationships.

All agreements in working relationships should be reached with a spirit of collaboration and a willingness to improve relationships between team members. Procedures should be established that permit future misunderstandings to be managed in more effective ways.

Preparation This part of the role-clarification activity can be done prior to the session or done first by each member of the team in private as the session begins. Each person should prepare answers to the following questions:

1. What do you feel the organization expects you to do to in your job? (This may include the formal job description.)
2. What do you actually do in your job? (Describe working activities and point out any discrepancies between your formal job description and your actual job activities.)
3. What do you need to know about other people's jobs that would help you do your work?
4. What do you think others should know about your job that would help them do their work?
5. What do you need others on the team to do in order for you to do your job the way you would like?
6. What do others on the team need you to do that would help them do their work?

The meeting will be more efficient if each team member shares with the other team members at least their answers to questions 1 and 2—what they expect of themselves (their roles and responsibilities)—with a written document before the team meets. This will allow other team members to review the expectations that other team members have of themselves before meeting to discuss as a team. They can then prepare their comments as to whether those are the expectations that they also have of that team member.

Meeting Design

Managing the role-clarification meeting is an important role for the team leader or facilitator. The following outlines the goals, ground rules, and the process to be followed.

Goals The goals of the role-clarification meeting should be presented, clarified, and discussed. Everyone should agree on the goals or hoped-for outcomes of the session(s). Typical goals include: improving team collaboration, better team problem solving, and better coordination to achieve group goals.

Ground Rules Ground rules should be developed by the team, written on a sheet of paper, and posted for all to see. Some suggested ground rules are as follows:

1. Be as candid and open as possible in a spirit of wanting to help improve the team.
2. If you want to know how another person feels or thinks about an issue, ask that person directly. If you are the person asked, give an honest response, even if it is to say, "I don't feel like responding right now."
3. If the meeting becomes unproductive for you, express this concern to the group.
4. Every member should have an opportunity to speak on every issue.
5. Decisions made should be agreeable to all those who are affected by the decision.

Clarifying Roles

Each person will have an opportunity to be the focal person and will follow these steps:

1. The focal person describes his or her job as he or she sees it. This means sharing all information about how the focal person understands the job: what is expected, when things are expected to be done, and how they are expected to be done. Other team members have the right to ask questions for clarification.

2. All others indicate that they understand what the focal person's position entails after this person's description: what is to be done, when things are to be done, and how they are to be done.

3. If the focal person and others have differences in expectations about the focal person's job, they should be resolved at this point so that there is a common agreement about what the focal person's job entails.

4. After agreement has been reached about the nature of the job, the focal person talks directly to each person on the team, identifying what he or she needs from the other in order to do the job as agreed on.

5. After getting requests for help from the focal person, the others on the team then have the opportunity to tell the focal person what they may need in return or what additional help the focal person might need from them so that the focal person can accomplish the demands of the position.

At the end of the role clarification session, it is often important to get feedback about how people are feeling. To get such feedback, team members might be asked to respond to the following questions:

1. How have you felt about the role clarification exercise?

2. What were the best parts for you?

3. What should be changed or improved in the future?

4. Do we need other sessions like this? If so, what should we discuss? When should we meet again?

The agreements made in the role clarification exercise should be written down and distributed to team members after the exercise in order to avoid any misunderstandings. This "memo of agreements" can then be referred to in future team meetings to ensure that team members are following through with their commitments. Figure 8.2 is an example of a short memo that was sent to a team after we facilitated a role-clarification exercise.

Figure 8.2 Role-Clarification Memo

MEMO

TO: ABC Team

FROM: Gibb Dyer

Even though I haven't received the notes from all of you yet, I think the following outlines the agreements made in our session last week. You should go over them in your regular meeting to make sure they are accurate.

Stephen (team leader)

1. Will meet with team members monthly on personal development issues.
2. Will invite team members to meetings with senior management when possible to get experience and will share information related to broader organizational issues/politics.
3. Share with Trey your perceptions of IT.
4. More timely feedback on comments on proposals that are sent out with a deadline.
5. Trey may need some resources to accomplish all his work—you will discuss this with him.
6. Stephen will find opportunities to delegate tasks when needed.

Sam

1. Create a transformation library.
2. More timely feedback on comments on proposals that are sent out with a deadline.
3. Will meet monthly with team generalists on development.
4. Will give feedback to Trey regularly.
5. Will put Alyssa on his team.

Trey

1. Will provide proactive analysis for key benchmark groups on a quarterly basis.
2. More timely feedback on comments on proposals that are sent out with deadlines for the team.
3. Will give feedback to Sam regularly.

Alyssa

1. Function to improve communication for the team.
2. Align team processes that directly or indirectly support the team.
3. Provide Sam with stop-start-continue feedback.
4. Give Sam weekly updates on the status of projects.
5. Share best practices with the team as a consultant.
6. More timely feedback on comments on proposals that are sent out with a clear deadline.
7. For Trey: Continue to have good data in his reports.

This type of team development meeting is one of the most productive interventions used to improve team effectiveness. Most groups of people slip into areas of ambiguity in their working relationships. Expectations about performance develop that people do not understand or even know about. For example, during a role-clarification exercise with one company's executive committee, the members of the president's management group were outlining their jobs as they saw them and identifying what they felt they needed from one another in order to carry out their jobs more effectively. When the human resource manager's turn came, she turned to the president and said, "One of the actions I need from you is a chance to get together with you a couple of times a year and review my performance and see what things you feel I need to do to improve."

The president asked in surprise, "Why do you need to get together with me?"

Responded the personnel manager, "When I was hired two years ago, it was my understanding that I was to report directly to you."

"Nobody ever cleared that with me," stated the president. "I thought you reported to the executive vice president."

The personnel manager had been waiting for two years for a chance to get direction from the person she thought was her direct superior, but that relationship had never been clarified until the role-clarification session. Although most work teams do not have misunderstood expectations to this degree, the periodic clarification of roles is useful for any work team.

Another role-clarification session we facilitated had a dramatic impact on the team and team leader. During the course of the session, the team members and the team leader—the company CEO—reached an impasse. The CEO believed his role was to make most of the decisions for the team, and the team members' role was mostly to follow his orders. Those on the team, the company vice presidents, reacted strongly against this view: they thought that decisions should be made more by consensus and that the role of the CEO should be to facilitate, not make, team decisions. The role clarification ended without resolution.

After the meeting, the vice presidents met and made a decision: either the CEO would need to rethink his role or they would quit. A few of the vice presidents, as representatives of the team, met with the board of directors, described the role conflicts between them and the CEO, and issued an ultimatum: "Either the CEO goes or we go." The board decided to "promote" the CEO to serve on the board and appointed one of the vice presidents to serve as the new CEO. As a result, the new management team began with clarity about the role of the CEO and began to perform at a much higher level than before.

Although the goal of such a team-building session is not to get the team leader fired or removed, a role-clarification session encourages the team to focus on the problems the leader has caused. Thus, the leader can respond in an affirmative way and agree to make some changes or, as in this case, stonewall the team and refuse to negotiate a new set of roles and behaviors. Either way, the exercise forces the team to confront some difficult issues and creates energy for change, which can lead to a more positive outcome for the team. Of course, this case also illustrates the risks involved when clarifying the roles of team members.

The Appreciative Inquiry Approach to Team Building

Up to this point we've focused on using a problem-centered approach to team building: the team identifies the problems it faces and then engages in problem solving to improve its performance. An alternative team-building approach is to focus on the more positive aspects of the team in a process called "appreciative inquiry" (AI).[1]

The AI approach to team building starts with the assumption that every team has some positive characteristics that can drive it to high performance. The issue for the team is how to discover and tap into these positive characteristics. Rather than focus on the negative—the problems that the team experiences—this approach focuses on the positive characteristics of the team. To begin the team-building activity, the manager, team leader, or consultant asks team members to answer the following questions:[2]

1. Think of a time when you were on a very successful team, a time that you felt energized, fulfilled, and the most effective—when you were able to accomplish even more than you imagined. What made it such a great team? Tell the story about the situation, the people involved, and how the team achieved its breakthrough.

2. Without being humble, what was it about you that contributed to the success of the team? Describe in detail these qualities and what you value about yourself that enables team success.

3. It is one year from today and our team is functioning more successfully than any of you imagined. What are we doing, how are we working together differently, what does this success look like, and how did we make it happen?

Members of the team pair up and share their answers to these questions. They then either move into larger subgroups and share their stories, or the entire team can be brought back together to report their stories and their feelings about the future of the team. Gervase Bushe, professor of leadership and organization development at Simon Fraser University, who uses the AI approach, explains how one team improved its performance through AI:

> In one business team I worked with one member talked about a group of young men he played pick-up basketball with and described why they were, in his opinion, such an outstanding "team." He described their shared sense of what they were there to do, lack of rigid roles, [and] easy adaptability to the constraints of any particular situation in the service of their mission. But what most captured the team's imagination was his description of how this group was both competitive and collaborative at the same time. Each person competed with all the rest to play the best ball, to come up with the neatest move and play. Once having executed it, and shown his

prowess, he quickly "gave it away" to the other players in the pick-up game, showing them how to do it as well. This was a very meaningful image for this group as a key, unspoken, tension was the amount of competitiveness members felt with each other at the same time as they needed to cooperate for the organization's good. "Back alley ball" became an important synthesizing image for this group that resolved the paradox of competitiveness and cooperation.[3]

By sharing such powerful images, a team may be able to envision a different way of functioning and create new values and beliefs that will enable it to plot a new course. The role of the team leader or consultant is to help the team identify images and metaphors that they can incorporate as they seek to improve team performance. The team members should ask and answer the following questions: (1) How can we as a team become like the high-performing teams that we've experienced in the past? and (2) How can I as a member of this team contribute to helping our team achieve its full potential? As the team and its members answer these questions, commitments are made to change the team in a positive direction. The team can use the images of team excellence to motivate the team to a higher level of performance.

The AI approach is often useful when team members tend to focus on the negative, continually bringing up negative images of the team and complaining about other team members. The positive approach of AI can give energy to an otherwise impotent and demoralized team. However, when using AI, the team should still be willing to confront important problems and to not see the world completely through rose-colored glasses.

Inter-team Team-Building Interventions

Because of the importance of dividing labor into various organizational units to promote efficiency, such units are and should be different. They have differing tasks, goals, personnel, time constraints, and structures, and therefore the functioning of these units is bound to be different. The issue is not how to make all units the same, but how to develop processes that allow these contrasting units to work together effectively. One strategy for bringing greater integration between work units is an inter-team development program using various interventions.

Diagnosing the Problem

An inter-team intervention may be considered when two or more teams, which must collaborate for each to achieve its own objectives, experience one or more of the following conditions:

- Team members avoid or withdraw from interactions with people from the other team when they should be spending more working time together.
- The mutual product or end result desired by both teams is delayed, diminished, blocked, or altered to the dissatisfaction of one or both parties.
- One team does not ask for services that they need from the other team.
- One team does not satisfactorily perform services needed by the other team.
- Team members feel resentment or antagonism as a result of interaction with the other team.
- Team members feel frustrated or rejected or that they are misunderstood by members of the other team with whom they must work.
- Team members spend more time either avoiding or circumventing interaction with the members of the other team or internally complaining about the other team than they spend working through mutual problems.

Designing the Solution

If at least one of the teams' managers is experiencing dysfunctional inter-team interaction, diagnoses the situation accurately, and is willing to contact the other team's manager, he or she may propose an inter-team development program. It is necessary to get the agreement of *both* teams to move the program ahead. If the leaders of the two teams agree to an inter-team development process, but do not get the commitment of their team members, team members are likely to put up a great deal of resistance to the program. The goal of the program is to develop a problem-solving process that will reduce the existing dysfunctional interaction and allow future problems to be solved more effectively before a breakdown in team interaction occurs. A number of design strategies can be used for planning and conducting the proposed program.

In preparation, the team leaders (or an outside facilitator or consultant) should explain the purpose and format of the program to members of both teams. Members of both teams should agree to participate.

Managers should set aside a block of time to get the appropriate people from both teams to work on the interface problems. If the two teams are small, it may be possible to involve all team personnel. If the teams are larger, it may be necessary to have representatives of the two teams work through the problem areas. The following describes some options for an inter-team building program.

Design A

1. Appropriate members from the two teams meet to work out a more functional method of operating. Members are introduced, and the plan, purpose, and schedule of the program are reviewed.

2. Ground rules are established. One essential ground rule is for people to adopt a problem-solving stance. The goal is to work out a solution, not to accuse or fix blame. Participants should agree to look at the behavior of their own team members and identify times when their own members are trying to accuse, fix blame, or defend a position rather than solve the problem.

3. Team members *in their own groups* answer the following questions and record their answers:
   a. What actions does the other team engage in that create problems for us? (List them.)
   b. What actions do we engage in that we think may create problems for them? (List them.)
   c. What recommendations would we make to improve the situation?

4. Each team brings its written answers and gives them to the other team to review.

5. Time is allotted for each team to review the work of the other team and to ask questions for clarification. Agreements and disparities in the two lists are noted.

6. Members of the two teams are now put into *mixed teams* composed of an equal number of members from both teams. Each mixed team reviews the lists and comes up with a list of the major problems or obstacles that they think keep the two teams from functioning together effectively. Each mixed team presents its list of problems to the whole group, and the results are tabulated. The whole group then identifies and lists what they think are the major problems.

7. Members return to the mixed teams. Each mixed team is asked to work out a recommended solution to one of the problems identified. Their recommendation should include what the problem is, what actions should be taken, who should be responsible for what actions, what the time schedule should be, and how to keep the problem from occurring again.

8. Mixed teams bring their solutions back to the whole group for review and to seek agreement, particularly from those who must implement the actions.

Design B This design is similar to design A, but is a "fishbowl" design. Instead of the two teams doing their work alone and then presenting the sheets to each other, each team discusses the problems *in front of* the other group.

1. Group X sits together in a circle. Group Y sits outside and observes and listens. Group X members discuss the three questions listed in item 3 of design A. A recorder writes down the points of discussion.
2. Group Y now moves into the center circle and repeats the process while group X observes and listens.
3. Following the fishbowl discussions, mixed teams are formed and perform the same tasks as in design A.

Design C A variation on designs A and B is to have the teams discuss different questions than those listed in design A. The designs for interaction are the same, but the questions are different, such as the following:

1. How do we see the other team? What is our image of them?
2. How do we think the other team sees us? What is their image of us?
3. Why do we see them the way we do?
4. Why do we think they see us as we think they do?
5. What would have to change so we would have a more positive image and interaction with each other?

Design D Another approach would involve the following steps:

1. An outside facilitator interviews members of both teams privately prior to the team-development session. He or she tries to identify the problems between the teams, the source of the problems, and potential solutions proposed by team members.
2. The facilitator summarizes the results of these interviews at the inter-team meeting. The summaries are printed or posted for all to see.
3. Mixed teams from both teams review the summary findings and list the major areas they feel need to be resolved. Major ideas are agreed on by the whole group.

4. Mixed teams devise recommended solutions to the problem assigned to them.

Design E This design involves selecting a mixed task force composed of members from both teams. The job of the task force is to review the interface problems and then recommend solutions to the problems for both groups to consider and agree on.

1. Representatives of the task force are selected in the following manner: Team X lists *all* its group members who the group feels could adequately represent them on the task force and gives this list to team Y. Team Y then selects three or four members from team X. Both teams engage in this listing and selecting process. The result is a mixed task force composed of members agreeable to both teams.

2. The task force may wish to either interview people from the other teams or invite a facilitator to work with it. Whatever the working style, the task force is asked to come up with the major conditions blocking inter-team effectiveness, what actions should be taken, who should be responsible for what actions, a time frame, how these problems can be prevented from occurring again, and what method will be used for solving other problems that may arise.

Follow-Up

What happens if the two teams have new or recurring problems in the future? There needs to be some method for dealing with new concerns as they arise and holding the teams accountable for prior agreements. It is possible to go through one of the five designs again. It is also possible to establish a review board made up of members of both groups. The function of this group is to examine the problem and come up with a recommended solution or procedure that would then be accepted by both teams. Then the teams need to agree on a process to review progress and take corrective action if necessary. This may take the form of a weekly or monthly meeting to track progress and ensure accountability.

Choosing an Appropriate Model

Given the variety of inter-team building interventions available, what determines which one would be most appropriate? One factor to consider is the confidence and competence of the team leaders to conduct such a program alone, without the help of an outside facilitator. If they choose to conduct the session alone, it would be wise to select an alternative that is simple, easy to communicate to others, and has minimal chance for slippage in implementation. Design E—the selection of an inter-team task force—is the most traditional way to work on the inter-team problems and is probably the easiest alternative to implement without help. It is also the design that has the least involvement of all the members of the two groups and may have the least impact, at least initially.

Design A probably is the most straightforward problem-solving format, with the least possibility of bringing conflicts and issues to the surface that could erupt into an unproductive rehash of old grievances. The fishbowl design may create reactions to individuals by the observers that may be difficult to handle without a trained facilitator. Similarly, approaching the issue through an examination of mutual images (design C) may also give rise to feelings and reactions that may be disruptive to one not used to handling such concerns.

To illustrate how an inter-team intervention might be used, we will present the case of one of our clients, ElectriCorp, an organization whose mission is to supply electric power to various locations within the United States.

ElectriCorp

To supply power to its customers, ElectriCorp relies on the performance of three "line crews" of five to ten men whose job it is to install high voltage power lines. Each crew is highly cohesive, led by a foreman. Moreover, crew members have worked together for many years and have an established pattern for doing their work and solving problems. The work is hard, dirty, and dangerous. Almost all of the men have had a friend who has been seriously injured or killed while on the job.

The crews typically work independently, but when there are large projects to complete, the crews must work together. This often creates serious conflicts, since the crews often don't agree with the other crews' approach to organizing and managing a particular job, and none of the three foremen want to be subservient to the others. Thus, when doing large projects together, the line crews tend to compete with one another, rather than cooperate.

On one project, the conflict became so nasty that one crew failed to inform another crew that the wires were "hot" at a certain section of the project. This serious safety breach was reported to senior management, who immediately launched an investigation. We, as consultants, were initially asked to serve as part of the team investigating the causes of the safety violations.

After the initial investigation, we were asked by ElectriCorp's senior management to "clean up the conflicts" between the crews. The approach we used to help the crews reduce their conflicts was a variation on Design A. All three crews were brought together in one room and the need for an inter-team development program was discussed. Each crew was asked to commit to solving the conflicts between themselves and the other crews and to agree to give the program a chance. Once this agreement was achieved, each crew was then asked to meet separately to list their perceptions of the other crews and the specific problems that they had in working with the other crews.

After meeting separately, the teams were brought back together and each crew reported its perceptions of the other crews. In our consulting role, we facilitated the discussion, making sure that each crew's perceptions were made clear and that each crew described the problematic behaviors of the other crews in concrete, specific terms. As a ground rule, crews were asked to be descriptive and avoid using emotionally laden language when critiquing the other crews. After each crew presented its perceptions of the other crews, the other crews could ask questions to clarify points that were made, but the crews were not allowed to debate the validity of the other crews' perceptions.

After each crew aired their views, the crews were then asked to come up with recommendations to improve the relationship between crews. Their suggestions were listed on large poster boards in the room. The crews discussed how they might do more advanced planning on the larger projects to determine who would do what and who would be in charge of the project. They also considered rotating crew members to better improve relationships between crews.

At the end of this inter-team session, each crew made a public commitment to change its behavior and implement the recommendations that were made. As a result of this intervention, the hostility between the crews did decrease and the crews now have a new approach to working with each other on large projects that minimizes the conflicts that they had in the past.

Notes

1. J. K. Cherney, "Appreciative Teambuilding: Creating a Climate for Great Collaboration," 2005, www.teambuildinginc.com/article_ai .htm.
2. Ibid.
3. Ibid.

9

TEAM BUILDING IN TEMPORARY, CROSS-CULTURAL, AND VIRTUAL TEAMS

Globalization, global corporations, and inter-company partnerships have changed the nature of teamwork for many teams. Indeed, in the twenty-first century more teams are being formed to pursue a short-term goal and an increasing number of teams are comprised of cross-cultural members. Moreover, an increasing percentage of teams are virtual teams that must collaborate across long distances.

Each type of team has its own unique characteristics and set of problems that need to be managed for the team to function effectively. Thus, different approaches to team building are needed, depending on the type of team. In this chapter we will examine how to apply the 5C model to three different types of teams: (1) the temporary team; (2) the cross-cultural team; and (3) the virtual team. For each team we will briefly describe the characteristics of the team, show how the 5C model applies to that particular type of team, and most importantly, discuss the kinds of team-building activities and interventions that we have found to have the most impact in improving team performance.

Managing the Temporary Team

The use of temporary teams, often called ad hoc committees, task forces, or project teams, is common in most organizations. At Cisco Systems they use the term *blast team* for this type of team. This collection of people must come together and in a relatively short time (usually from six weeks to a year) come up with a work plan, make decisions, develop recommendations, or take specific actions that are carefully thought through and useful. To accomplish these goals with people who already have full-time assignments elsewhere in the organization, the team must quickly coalesce and be productive almost immediately—which is not easy given that developing the appropriate team context, composition, and team competencies typically takes considerable time.

Temporary teams are, by definition, together for a short duration, and consequently team members may feel that there is little time or need for team development activities. They often feel under pressure to dive immediately into the work at hand and are reluctant to spend the time needed to get acquainted, plan how the group will work together, develop measurable performance goals, and build some commitment to one another. The following discussion outlines how a temporary team should manage the 5Cs to achieve maximum performance.

Context Issues for Temporary Teams

An important context condition is to give the temporary team adequate resources and authority to get the work done. A few years ago, a major U.S. automobile company found itself behind its competitors in important design features. An analysis showed that temporary design teams made up of people from several basic functional departments (engineering, R&D, production, and so on) took as much as a year longer than competitors to come up with new designs. Further analysis also disclosed that most team members were told by their superiors in their functional departments, "Don't you make any final decisions until you come back and check with me." This meant that decisions in the design team were continually being postponed while team members checked back with functional bosses. These delays continued until the design teams were eventually given authority to make key decisions without checking back with departments.

While having the proper amount of authority to make decisions is important, temporary teams are typically acting at the request of senior managers in the organization, and it is senior management who often has the final word when it comes to the decisions or actions that the team takes. Hence, it is important for the team to keep senior managers or anyone else who is sponsoring the team activities aware of the progress the team is making and what decisions have been or will be made. Some teams use the RACI model to ensure that the team clearly identifies who is *Responsible* for carrying out which activities, who is *Accountable* to ensure activities are performed up to the desired standards and goals are met, who needs to be *Consulted* before certain decisions can be made, and finally who needs to be *Informed* when decisions are made or milestones are reached. Spelling this out when the temporary team is formed can facilitate the efficient delivery of work with appropriate oversight and governance.

Composition Issues

It is important for the team leader to make sure that members in a temporary team: (a) have the skills needed to complete the task, (b) see the team as an important priority for them, and (c) have the time needed to complete their team tasks and work with the team to help it succeed. We've found it helpful for a temporary team, when it first meets, to have team members rate themselves on a scale of 1 to 10 on how much of a priority the team is and time (hours per week) they have for the team. The exercise for determining priorities and time is as follows:

1. Put the name of each member of the team horizontally on the whiteboard and put the words *priority* and *time* vertically, on the far-left side, below their names. Then have each person on the team rate themselves from 1 to 10 in terms of the priority the team has for them and also list the average number of hours per week the person can spend working for the team.

2. Summarize the priority rankings and the time commitments. Note the range of times and priorities and the averages for the two dimensions.

3. In the group, let each person who desires explain his or her priority and time rankings and then come to agreement as to a realistic amount of time and energy that can be expected of the team as a whole. Those with a higher priority and team commitments may be allowed to accept heavier assignments. Making this decision openly reduces the resentment some have for doing more work and the guilt of others for letting them.

4. In some instances, those team members who may not have the time or see the team as a priority may need to be dropped from the team. Prior meetings before team assignments should have uncovered this, but sometimes priorities and time commitments can change and so adjustments need to be made.

We've also found that it is helpful to have team members rate each other in terms of their contribution to team performance at the end of the project. When team members know that others will rate their contribution and that this will be used in performance appraisals then it creates an incentive to contribute to team performance.

Competency Issues

In temporary teams, it's particularly important for them to have competencies in: (1) setting goals, (2) solving problems, (3) making decisions, (4) ensuring follow-through and completion of tasks, and (5) establishing open lines of communication.

Developing these competencies helps to establish guidelines for how the team will function. Provisions also need to be formulated for changing the guidelines if they prove to be dysfunctional or inappropriate as conditions change. The guidelines should also clarify actions and roles to reduce any ambiguity or mixed expectations of people as to how things ought to function, which is the basis of a great deal of conflict in a temporary team.

To clarify expectations and create norms for openness and sharing, the following questions should be raised in the first temporary team meeting. The team leader should give each team member five minutes to think about and respond to the following questions:

- What worries you most or is your biggest concern about working on this team?
- How would this team function if everything went just as you hoped?
- What do you expect to be the barriers to effective team functioning? What will likely prevent the team from achieving its goals?
- What actions do you think must be taken to ensure the positive outcomes?

Each person should be given an opportunity to share reactions, and everyone should respond to each question in turn. Try to identify the major concerns people have and list them on a whiteboard or flipchart. These concerns should become items on a planning agenda as conditions to take into consideration in order to ensure a positive outcome.

Other questions that might be explored include:

1. What are our goals and are they realistic given our other commitments?
2. How will we make decisions?
3. How will assignments for individual team members be made?
4. How will we track our progress?
5. How will be resolve conflicts that emerge?
6. How will we hold people accountable for their role on the team?
7. How will we know when we've achieved our goal?

Answers to these questions and the team expectations should be summarized and shared with the team. This sets the groundwork for moving forward effectively as a temporary team. Too often, such teams move immediately to starting on the project rather than setting the ground rules that are needed for the team to be effective. We've found that spending the first session determining the level of commitment to the team and setting clear expectations prevents many problems that occur as they start working together.

Change

Given the short time frame that temporary teams work together, changes need to be made quickly if the team gets off track and is not performing well. Thus, periodic start-stop-continue sessions are especially helpful for the temporary team (probably once every two to four weeks—depending on the time frame for the team). Also, if the team is going to function over several months, after four weeks it would be helpful to have a role-clarification exercise to ensure that team members clearly understand their own role as well as the roles of others on the team.

Team Leadership

Leadership in temporary teams requires the leader to have the ability (or get help from the outside) to help team members get to know each other and feel a connection to the team and its goals. The team leader also facilitates setting the ground rules for team collaboration and functioning that we have just discussed. Temporary team leaders also need to spend significant time keeping members of the team informed on both their individual assignments and the progress of the team. This is due to that fact that team members can get distracted by their other priorities (when team participation involves only a part-time commitment). The team leader needs to set up a clear protocol for sharing team information (e.g. Google docs) and scheduling team meetings to resolve team issues and problems. The team leader is also responsible for procuring the resources needed by the team—which is often not easy since many organizations don't budget additional resources for temporary teams. Moreover, the team leader needs to keep key stakeholders informed and involved—particularly senior managers who may have authorized the creation of the temporary team—so they will not be surprised with the team's timeline and will be satisfied with the results.

Creating Effective Cross-Cultural Teams

One of the more dramatic changes in teams in recent years has been the increasing number of teams composed of members from different cultural backgrounds. Various studies of cross-cultural teams present contradictory findings. Some studies indicate that cross-cultural teams can be highly creative and high performing while others show that such teams have significant conflicts and low performance.[1] In fact, both seem to be true. When a team is composed of individuals who have different norms, values, language, and experiences, the likelihood of creative problem solving is enhanced, but the chances for misunderstandings, mistrust, and miscommunication also increase.

Because members of a cross-cultural team may lack specific information about each other, they often form stereotypical expectations of each team member based on their prior experience or history with people from that country, ethnicity, or culture of origin. For example, because Javier is from Mexico or Jean François is from France, team members will expect them to behave according to the stereotypes they have of people from Mexico or France. Such stereotypes often undermine the team's ability to perform at a high level since they create mismatched expectations and unwanted conflicts. Research has shown that culture has a significant impact on a person's assumptions regarding: (1) the role of the individual in the team, (2) power and authority, (3) uncertainty, and (4) time. Table 9.1 describes how different assumptions concerning these factors might influence team members.[2]

Table 9.1 Cultural Variables that Influence Multicultural Teams

Variable	Implications for Multicultural Teams
Individualism versus collectivism *Individualism:* prefer to act and be recognized as individuals rather than as members of groups (the United States, France, the United Kingdom, Germany) *Collectivism:* prefer to act as members of groups (China, Japan, Indonesia, West Africa)	• Individualistic team members will voice their opinions more readily, challenging the direction of the team. The opposite is true of collectivists. Collectivists prefer to consult colleagues more than do individualists before making decisions. • Collectivists don't need specific job descriptions or roles but will do what is needed for responsibility for tasks and may need reminding that they are part of a team. • Individual-oriented team members prefer direct, constructive feedback on their performance tied closely to their individual performance. Collectivists might feel embarrassed if singled out for praise or an individual incentive award. • Collectivists prefer face-to-face meetings. Individualists prefer to work alone, not needing face-to-face contact.
Power distance *High distance:* prefer and accept that power is not distributed equally (France and Russia) *Low distance:* prefer and accept that power is distributed more equally (the Netherlands, the United States)	• Team members from cultures that value equality (that is, low power distance) expect to use consultation to make key decisions, and subordinates are more likely to question and challenge leaders or authority figures. • A team leader exercising a more collaborative style might be seen as weak and indecisive by team members from a high-power-distance culture. • Members from high-power-distance cultures will be very uncomfortable communicating directly with people higher in the organization.

Table 9.1 (*Continued*)

Variable	*Implications for Multicultural Teams*
Uncertainty avoidance	
High-uncertainty-avoidance cultures: prefer more structured tasks and avoid ambiguity (France, Japan, Russia) *Low-uncertainty-avoidance cultures:* have a high tolerance for ambiguity and risk taking (the United States, Hong Kong)	• In a culture in which risk taking is the norm or valued, team members tend to be comfortable taking action or holding meetings without much structure or formality. Members who are more risk averse need a clearer, prepared meeting structure, perhaps with formal presentation by all members of the team. They're unlikely to take an active part in brainstorming sessions. • Members from lower-avoidance cultures do not respond well to micromanagement. They may also be more willing to use new technologies.
Task or relationship orientation *Long-term orientation:* China, Japan *Short-term orientation:* the United States, Russia	• Team members from long-term-oriented cultures want to spend extra social time together, building trust, and may have problems interacting smoothly with short-term-oriented members. They also like opportunities to work toward long-term goals. • Individuals from long-term-oriented cultures demonstrate greater concern for relationships, whereas those from short-term-oriented cultures demonstrate greater concern for task completion.

Source: Adapted from G. Hofstede, *Culture's Consequences: International Differences in Work-Related Values* (Thousand Oaks, CA: Sage, 1980).

Applying the 5Cs to Cross-Cultural Teams

These four categories of cultural assumptions (and others too numerous to discuss here) explain why cross-cultural teams often have difficulty. First, people from different cultures interpret the world differently. From one cultural perspective, a certain act, a word, or an object may be entirely appropriate, but from another cultural perspective, it may be highly offensive. Different assumptions held by team members can lead to miscommunication and conflict. To remedy these problems, we find that using the 5C model of team performance can help to ensure the success of a cross-cultural team.

Context

Creating the right context for a cross-cultural team is critical. The agenda for the initial team meeting should be similar to that for temporary teams described previously. The team members need to discuss the importance and priority of the team; share their expectations for the team; clarify the goals of the team; and formulate operating guidelines for issues regarding decision making, work assignments, raising concerns, resolving conflicts, and so forth. Significant upfront, face-to-face time can be especially important for cross-cultural teams so that individuals can appreciate the similarities and differences of team members, and this can be discussed among team members.

To help build mutual trust and understanding, some cross-cultural teams have found it valuable to administer an online version of the Myers-Briggs Type Indicator, the widely used personality assessment tool that places people in one of four personality dimensions. (See humanmetrics.com for an online version of the test.) All team members should understand what each member brings to the team. At the team kickoff meeting, the team can review each team member's personality profile and background, and the team leader can encourage members to share some information about their country, culture, or personal background that might be useful knowledge for other team members. It sometimes helps if team members agree to remind each other of their own personality styles when they speak. For example, someone from a culture that values verbal expression might say, "As you know, I tend to think out loud," or, "Please remind me not to take up too much airtime." These kinds of conversations prove to be invaluable for helping team members view each other as individuals. Naturally, this is critical to the formation of trust among team members.

Another way to build trust and mutual understanding is through a teamwork activity as part of the team's first meeting. One such activity is the "desert survival" activity, in which the team must work together to figure out how to survive in the desert. Try to have an opening activity that is fun, interesting, and interactive rather than competitive. After the exercise, the team leader should consider asking team members to say something about their country and culture and how it tends to influence their work style. Team members can use concrete examples from the exercise just completed to help others understand their approach to teamwork and problem solving. At the end of the exercise, each team member could list on a whiteboard some of the questions, puzzles, or conflicts they had with other team members. The team could then explore how to help each team member understand what cultural rules (or other factors) may have caused the discomfort and discuss what be done in the future to avoid such problems.

Another approach to clarify cultural differences would be to have the team engage in an appreciative inquiry team exercise described in Chapter 8. As team members describe their most productive team experiences and the role they played on the team, cultural differences can be identified and clarified by team members whose experience in productive teams may be quite different. We often see individuals from Asian countries describe their successful teams as ones where the team leader makes most of the decisions and roles are well-defined.

Americans, in contrast, often cite teams where there was a lot of freedom and little structure as being their best team experience. Such differences in expectations need to be reconciled for a cross-cultural team to perform effectively.

Composition

Creating a successful cross-cultural team requires several important things regarding the composition of the team. In additional to choosing team members who have the skills, experience, and motivation to help the team succeed, team members should be selected on the basis of their ability to communicate in a common language. Certainly it's possible to use interpreters, but the process is slow and unwieldy. Case studies have shown that inadequate proficiency in a common language results in misunderstandings and mistakes that impede team performance. Moreover, those members of the team who are less proficient at the most common team language (typically English) are often deemed by other team members to be less competent. Not surprisingly, this inhibits their ability to contribute to the team. Thus, clarifying what language will be the primary language for the team—Chinese, French, English, or something else—and making sure each team member is proficient in the language is important. If the team leader and other team members are multilingual, so much the better, for they can help clarify misunderstandings that may occur. Furthermore, finding team members who have lived and worked in other countries or have previously worked on cross-cultural teams is helpful for team success.

Competencies

One of the advantages of cross-cultural teams is that team members bring a diverse set of experiences, values, and beliefs that can be helpful to team performance. In fact, the cross-cultural team gives the team the opportunity to create a unique culture composed of cultural rules that fit the particular task of the team. Early on in the team's development, the team leader should lead a discussion of each of the competencies listed in Chapter 4 and discuss how each team member feels such competencies might be developed in the team.

A discussion of these competencies also creates opportunities to talk about and clarify cultural differences. For example, a discussion in the team regarding how a team meeting should be run would likely raise a number of important issues to be resolved as team members from different cultures who have experienced different meeting styles begin to work together. Moreover, the focus on developing these competencies needs to be done early in the development of the team. Neal Goodman emphasizes the importance of early, competency-building activities on cross-cultural teams:

> Those who work on global teams need to go through a cross-cultural teambuilding program in the formative stages of team development to avoid misunderstandings and to establish team trust. It is critical that team members explore the cultural nuances that often undermine global team effectiveness. This conversation might include: team members' perceptions of country cultures and customs; setting global standards of roles, responsibility, and accountability; leadership and management styles; discussion of virtual and face-to-face communication styles; and the development of a communication plan. Other relevant topics to be covered should include the cultural tendencies of all relevant countries and how these impact teamwork.[3]

Change

Early in their development, cross-cultural teams need to regularly assess how they are performing so that they can quickly make any needed course corrections. This could be as simple as taking time after each meeting to critique the meeting's effectiveness or having a weekly or biweekly "stop-start-continue" team-building session to address problems on the team. Role clarification can also be a useful team-building activity in the first week or two after the team has been working together.

Violated expectations as a result of different cultural rules are often the cause of conflict in cross-cultural teams. There are three primary ways that expectations tend to be violated:

- Communication behaviors
- Decision-making processes
- Conflict resolution behaviors and processes

In the area of communication behaviors, the specific potential areas of conflict include how quickly to respond to other team member requests, what communication vehicle to use for different types of information, and how to communicate sensitive information. It is important for the team to establish expectations regarding these issues at the beginning of the project. Otherwise, it is easy for conflict to arise when communication norms or expectations are violated.

In one cross-cultural team we worked with, the leader had a team member who simply stopped communicating for three weeks. The leader sent repeated e-mails requesting information, to which the member did not reply. Rather than get angry at him, thinking maybe there were extenuating circumstances, the team leader consciously made an effort to keep the lines of communication open. She called him and said, "Please tell me if I have offended you." He said, "Well, I'm a Yorkshire man, and we go quiet when we are thinking." The team leader was astounded. She felt like saying, "I don't care if you come from Mars, I need the stuff."

This team leader realized that it would have been helpful if she had clearly established expectations at the beginning of team formation that members should expect to respond to each other's e-mails or requests within a specific time period (within 48 hours is a typical expectation unless the nature of the task requires faster—or allows for slower—responses).

A second area for which it is important to establish expectations is decision-making processes. It is important for all team members to clearly understand how decisions will be made, as well as their role in the process. In some cultures and organizations, the leader of the team usually makes the decision after listening to the issues that team members raise. In more collectivist and egalitarian decision-making cultures, decisions are made by consensus after continuing discussions among team members. The team leader plays an important facilitator role in this process, ensuring that all voices are listened to and that the team comes to an agreement on a decision. It is often helpful at the beginning of the project for the team to discuss and agree on the processes that will be used for decision making. It is especially important to anticipate how final decisions will be made if there is disagreement among the team as to what the decision should be.

A third area for which it is important to establish expectations is conflict resolution behaviors and processes. The basic idea is to establish some ground rules in case of disagreements among team members or with the team leader regarding how those differences of opinion will be handled and resolved. Some individuals feel perfectly comfortable expressing differences of opinion with other members of the team and engaging in direct disagreements and dialogue about those disagreements. Others feel very uncomfortable openly disagreeing with other members of a team and prefer to use more subtle processes for expressing disagreements. For example, in the United States, individuals tend to prefer to confront a problem directly with another individual, even if it is the team leader. In most Asian cultures, direct confrontation is avoided at all costs. When a subordinate wants to give feedback to a boss, this is typically done only in a roundabout way through the grapevine (other members of the team), and often when the team is out at night together drinking. This allows conflicts to be resolved in more subtle, informal ways without direct confrontation during team meetings or discussions.

In summary, developing an effective cross-cultural team is not easy. It requires creating a context that encourages people on the team to be sensitive to the different values of team members. It requires the team to find a common language to communicate in along with developing competencies for sharing information and managing conflict. Certain team interventions to clarify roles and expectations can be very helpful. But the team leader is often the key to providing the support and guidance a cross-cultural team needs.

Collaborative Leadership

The leader of a cross-cultural team needs to be sensitive to cultural differences and attuned to the fact that his or her own cultural values may be inconsistent with those of other members of the team.[4]

Thus, team leaders who have had experience in working overseas or in a multicultural environment will more likely be successful in helping lead such a team. Moreover, if the team leader has facility in the languages of team members, that certainly is a plus. Talking to persons in their own language tends to put them at ease, and they will often be more willing to be open and share their true feelings. However, in situations where the team leader does not speak a team member's language, the team leader may need to use a competent interpreter when speaking with a team member to allow that person to share their issues and concerns in their own language. A competent interpreter can be a valuable tool for helping the team leader effectively communicate with a team member who is not proficient in the leader's language. A skilled interpreter can also provide guidance to the team leader in understanding cultural differences that may influence a team member's behavior and performance.

Leaders of cross-cultural teams need to be aware that some miscommunication is inevitable. As a result, they need to pay careful attention to clarifying expectations and repeating communications than might be done otherwise. Having all decisions written down and disseminated to the team in a timely manner, as well has writing down ground rules for the team and sharing minutes of team meetings, is particularly important. Even when people share the same language, it's not unusual to have people leave a team meeting with different expectations about what is to happen next. Thus, the leader of a cross-cultural team will generally have to spend significantly more one-on-one time meeting with team members to understand their concerns and developing processes to share written communications about the team, team meetings, and team progress to avoid misunderstandings.

Building Effective Virtual Teams

Only a few years ago virtual teams were rare. Today they are commonplace. What has changed? First, companies are increasingly global, with office locations in numerous countries. Second, advances in communication technology have dramatically lowered the costs of coordinating across distances, thereby making it more cost-effective to create and manage virtual teams. Finally, companies face increasingly complex business problems that require the contributions of people with varied knowledge who reside in different locations and time zones.

Virtual teams differ from traditional teams in at least four ways:

1. Greater diversity in work norms and expectations
2. Team members living in different times zones, making it more difficult to find common times to communicate directly
3. Greater reliance on technology as a vehicle for communication
4. Greater demands on the team leader

Unlike traditional co-located teams, virtual teams are assembled with individuals from different locations with much greater diversity of cultures, languages, and business functions (e.g. sales and engineering). Because a virtual team is typically composed of members with much greater individual diversity, there is much greater diversity in team work norms and expectations.

A major difference between virtual and traditional teams is that virtual teams cannot rely on face-to-face meetings and must communicate using a much wider variety of technologies. The members of a virtual team can choose from a range of communication technologies to coordinate team activities, including e-mail, electronic displays or whiteboards, bulletin boards or web pages (including team calendars and chat rooms), teleconference (audio or video), or multipoint multimedia technology (a combination of full-motion video, whiteboard, and audio links).

Context

To create the right context for a virtual team means identifying and using the right technologies to help team members communicate, solve problems, and get their work done. The majority of effective virtual teams use technology to simulate reality by creating virtual workspaces that are accessible to everyone at any time. These are more than networked drives with shared files. Rather they are workspaces where the group is reminded of its mission, work plan, decisions, and working documents.

A good example of a virtual team workspace is one that was set up at Shell Chemicals by team leader Tom Coons, who led a project to develop a companywide cash-focused approach to financial management.[5] The team's virtual workspace, essentially a website accessed on an intranet, prominently displayed the project's mission statement on its home page, as well as the photographs and names of team members in a clocklike arrangement. The home page also had links to other tabs, or "walls," each devoted to a particular aspect of the project. The tab labeled "people," for instance, kept not only individuals' contact information but also extensive profiles that included their accomplishments, areas of expertise, and interests, as well as information about other stakeholders. On a tab labeled "purpose" was a hierarchical listing of the mission statement, the goals, and the tasks for meeting the goals, indicating how close each task was to completion. The "meeting center" wall contained all the information needed to manage the teleconferences: notices of when they were being held, who was supposed to come, agendas, and minutes. Yet another wall displayed the team's entire work product, organized into clearly numbered versions so that people would not inadvertently work on the wrong one. The team room kept information current, organized, and easily accessible. This type of virtual workspace creates a team identity, generates commitment to the team, and helps the team stay organized.

The Shell team created these tools internally. But an increasing number of collaboration tools like this are relatively inexpensive or even free. For example, Salesforce.com offers Chatter, software that creates collaboration tools for teams and organizations. Chatter takes the best of Facebook and Twitter and applies it to enterprise collaboration. It uses new ways of sharing information like "feeds" and "groups" so that without any effort, people can see what individuals and teams are focusing on, how projects are progressing, and what deals are closing. It can change the way teams collaborate on product development, customer acquisition, and content creation by making it easy for everyone to see what everyone else is doing. At companies using Chatter, e-mail inboxes have shrunk dramatically (by 43% at Salesforce.com) because many communications take place through status updates and feeds in Chatter. "Employees now follow accounts and updates are automatically broadcast to them in real-time via Chatter," Salesforce founder Marc Benioff told us. "This is the true power of Chatter—bringing to light the most important people and ideas that move our companies forward. I call this social intelligence, and it's giving everyone access to the people, the knowledge, and the insight they need to make a difference."[6]

Some studies have found that these types of virtual workspaces are far better than e-mail for coordinating virtual teams.[7] Indeed, many virtual teams have found that e-mail is a poor way for teams as a whole to collaborate. Trying to do the main work of the team through one-to-one exchanges between members can cause those not included to feel left out. To avoid this mistake, some teams have adopted the practice of copying everyone on every e-mail exchange between members, and soon everyone in the team is drowning in messages. To cope, many team members simply resort to deleting e-mails without reading them. Over time this can create significant communication problems among team members when some have communicated information that others have not read or understood. A virtual workspace tends to be a far better way to organize team meetings and work. A key benefit of the virtual workspace is that it maintains an ongoing record for the team that enables virtual team members to understand the context of information as they see other members sharing the information. It also keeps an ongoing record of decisions, tasks completed, and progress toward the team's final deliverable.

A virtual workspace helps the team members exchange data, revise working documents, and stay organized, but it is not the best method for coordinating more complex team interactions, such as brainstorming, debating and prioritizing options, or developing a common understanding of complex concepts, process flows, or scenarios. For these more complex tasks, the group must rely on audio- or videoconferences. (Table 9.2 provides a summary of the types of tasks virtual teams face and the communication methods available to the team.)

Audioconferences are much better than e-mail, web pages, or bulletin boards for brainstorming, defining problems, prioritizing and voting on ideas, stating and discussing opinions, and reaching simple compromises. But audioconferences are also difficult to facilitate because the team leader must be very sensitive to not only what is being said but how it is being said. Indeed, effective team leaders typically follow up with individual team members after the conference call to make sure they felt listened to and understood.

In some cases, the team members must discuss and debate complex concepts that may involve diagrams of process flows, sketches of products or blueprints, or other visual data. The more complex the task and the greater the interdependence of team members, the more important it is to use videoconferencing technology such as Skype to simulate face-to-face interactions. For a simultaneous video- or audioconference, along with the ability to display data or graphics on a computer, Webex and Zoom conferencing have become popular tools for coordinating the work of virtual teams. Finding the right technology for the job (task) that needs to be done by the team is critical for ensuring that a virtual team is completing its tasks as efficiently and effectively as possible.

Composition

Virtual teams must communicate long distance, which means team members must understand how and when to use particular communication technologies. Thus, team members must be chosen based on their ability to use the needed technologies or be willing to be trained to use those technologies. Also, team members in virtual teams need to feel comfortable working alone and not need face-to-face contact on a regular basis. Virtual team leaders should keep this in mind when selecting who should be on the team.

Table 9.2 Matching Virtual Team Tasks and Communication Methods

Communication Modes, Listed from Least Expensive to Most Expensive	Generating Ideas and Plans and Collecting Data	Benefits of and Problems with Answers	Benefits of and Problems Without Answers	Negotiating Technical or Interpersonal Conflicts
E-mail, web pages, and bulletin boards (data only)	*Good for:* exchanging data; revising plans and documents; commenting on ideas, products, polling, and son on *Not good for:* brainstorming, prioritizing, voting on ideas, reaching consensus	*Good for:* defining problems, transmitting data, and analyzing data *Not good for:* reaching consensus on problems, prioritizing data, discussing the data analysis	*Good for:* identifying options *Not good for:* debating options, prioritizing options, making decisions or judgments	*Good for:* stating opinions *Not good for:* discussing opinions, reaching compromises, resolving conflicts, deciding alternatives
Audioconference	*Good for:* brainstorming, prioritizing and voting on ideas, reaching consensus *Not good for:* depicting complex concepts, process flows, scenarios, or sketches	*Good for:* defining problems, prioritizing options, making straightforward decisions *Not good for:* displaying and diagramming data, performing in-depth and complex analysis	*Good for:* discussing options, making assignments *Not good for:* making judgments about ambiguous topics	*Good for:* stating and discussing opinions, deciding among straightforward options or solutions, reaching simple compromises *Not good for:* resolving interpersonal conflict or disagreement

Table 9.2 (Continued)

Communication Modes, Listed from Least Expensive to Most Expensive	Generating Ideas and Plans and Collecting Data	Benefits of and Problems with Answers	Benefits of and Problems Without Answers	Negotiating Technical or Interpersonal Conflicts
Videoconference	Good for: brainstorming, sketching ideas, drawing concepts, gaining agreement on complex concepts, process flows, scenarios or sketches	Good for: displaying and analyzing data, discussing trends	Good for: listing options, debating and prioritizing options, making decisions	Good for: discussing opinions, reaching compromises, deciding among alternative solutions, resolving simple interpersonal disagreement Not good for: resolving complex interpersonal conflict or disagreement.

Source: Adapted from D. L. Duarte and N. T. Snyder, *Mastering Virtual Teams*, 3rd ed. (San Francisco: Josey-Bass, 2006).

Competencies

The competencies that should be emphasized by virtual team leaders are as follows:

- Setting clear goals as a team
- Being clear about roles and assignments
- Creating an effective virtual decision-making process
- Building trust on the team
- Creating open communications channels
- Developing processes to manage conflict

The team leader should be aware that these are key competencies needed for a virtual team to succeed and thus should provide training on these competencies (see Chapter 4) or engage in other team-building activities to instill these competencies in the team.

Change

The logistics of managing change in a virtual team and implementing traditional team-building approaches are certainly a challenge. To improve team performance virtual teams can:

- Assess the context and composition of the team as the team is formed. To a large extent, the context of a virtual team is not particularly conducive to effective teamwork: the structure, technology, reward systems, and so on might not encourage collaboration. Moreover, individuals on virtual teams often have different cultural backgrounds that can make teamwork challenging. Thus, if possible, the team should engage in some of the development activities designed for cross-cultural teams described earlier in this chapter. By so doing, the team should be able to recognize the context barriers that could make teamwork difficult and develop plans of action to respond to those barriers. The team should also discuss if it has the requisite knowledge and skills on the team to complete its task.

- Periodically assess its performance by filling out the team-building checklist in Chapter 5. Data from the checklist can then be shared with the team online or by videoconferencing, and the team can then identify and address team problems. After identifying and prioritizing the team's issues and problems, the team leader might select one of the team-building techniques presented in previous chapters, recognizing that the format would likely need to be adapted to a virtual team (although we encourage face-to-face team-building sessions when possible).

Because of the increasing use of virtual teams in today's organizations, we believe that team building in these types of teams will become increasingly important in the future. For organizations to be competitive they will need to be attuned to the needs of their virtual teams and provide appropriate training and resources in order for them to succeed.

Collaborative Leadership

By now it should be somewhat obvious that the demands on the team leader are much greater on a virtual team. In addition to the team leader skills described in Chapter 6, virtual team leaders must have enough cross-cultural and cross-functional experience to be aware of potential conflicts in work norms and expectations. Moreover, they not only must be aware of the areas of potential conflict but must educate team members about these differences and help the team establish a set of commonly understood and agreed-on work norms and expectations. Team leaders must also be proficient with the use of a variety of communication technologies, knowing both how and when to use them. In addition, they must put in extra time preparing, and making sure team members are prepared for, team meetings so that team interactions can be as productive as possible. Finally, they must communicate frequently on an individual basis with each team member. These side conversations are critical to resolving disagreements, negotiating compromises, and making sure each member feels understood and heard by the leader.

The demands of managing a virtual team exceed the demands of traditional teams. This means that the role of team leader is crucial and is much more challenging than this person's role in traditional teams. Although team membership may be part-time, team leadership is often more than full time. A rule of thumb that we suggest is that *the team leader should allocate 50 percent more time to the project than he or she would be spending managing a co-located team working on a similar problem.* There are two primary reasons that team leaders must spend significantly more time managing virtual teams. First, the team leader (or assistant) must organize all team meetings and team activities electronically. This tends to be more time intensive because these communications must be clearly spelled out, often through written communication.

Second, effective virtual team leaders have frequent phone conversations with individual members to probe into their real feelings, questions, and suggestions for more effective team functioning. This gives the team leader an opportunity to keep his or her finger on the pulse of the team. Effective virtual team leaders know they must devote extra time to monitoring the morale of team members and concerns they may have with other team members or the team leader.

Notes

1. E. B. Magnus, "The Conceptualization of Social Complexity in Global Teams," *Nordic Psychology* 63 (2011): 35.
2. G. Hofstede, *Culture's Consequences: International Differences in Work-Related Values* (Thousand Oaks, CA: Sage, 1980).
3. N. Goodman, "Cultivating Cultural Intelligence," *Training* 48 (March–April 2011): 38.
4. D. J. Pauleen, "Leadership in a Global Virtual Team: An Action Learning Approach," *Leadership and Organization Development Journal* 24 (2003): 157.

5. This example of a virtual workspace is taken from A. Majchrzak, A. Malhotra, J. Stamps, and J. Lipnack, "Can Absence Make a Team Grow Stronger?" *Harvard Business Review* 82, no. 5 (May 2004): 134–135.

6. J. Dyer, H. Gregersen, and C. M. Christensen, *The Innovator's DNA: Mastering the Five Skills of Disruptive Innovators* (Boston: Harvard Business Review Press, 2011), 44.

7. Ibid.

10

TEAM BUILDING IN ALLIANCE, ENTREPRENEURIAL, AND FAMILY TEAMS

Continuing our discussion of team building in different types of teams, in this chapter we will explore how to apply team-building principles to alliance teams, entrepreneurial (start-up) teams, and family teams. These types of teams are increasingly important and require an understanding of their unique characteristics and how teamwork is necessary for them to be effective.

Interorganizational Alliance Teams

Alliances between organizations now count for a significant percentage of revenue in many corporations. Thus, "alliance teams" comprised of team members from each organization are being formed in greater numbers than ever before. But the challenges that these teams face are formidable. Indeed, most studies on alliances show that 30 to 50 percent fail to meet the objectives outlined by the alliance team at the beginning of the alliance.[1] Such failures are largely due to: (1) differences in partner cultures (this may be due to differences in corporate culture but also may be due to differences in national cultures), (2) incompatible partner objectives, (3) poor alliance leadership, and (4) poor integration processes.[2] Each of these is related to a failure in managing the alliance team rather than a "failure in technology" or "changes in the business environment," two factors that clearly can derail an alliance but are largely beyond the control of the partners. In short, the number-one reason that alliances fail is an inability to manage the alliance team effectively.

Alliance teams differ from typical internal teams in at least five important ways:

1. Alliance team members come from organizations with different cultures and values.
2. Alliance team members work for different organizations with different goals and consequently they can have difficulty agreeing on common goals.
3. Due in part to divergent organizational goals, trust is a significant issue in almost all alliance teams.
4. Decision making in alliance teams is often complex and confusing because it can be unclear who has the power to make decisions.
5. Alliance teams often have people from each organization that have some similar skills and functional background. Thus, there is generally a duplication of skills among team members and there can be conflict over who is "right" when addressing issues. This also tends to make the teams quite large and unwieldy.

In this section we will describe how one organization, Eli Lilly, has come up with a process that creates the right context, composition, competencies, collaborative leadership, and change practices to develop effective alliance teams.

Managing Alliance Teams: Lessons from Eli Lilly and Company

Eli Lilly and Company is among a small number of companies that have distinguished themselves as leaders in the management of strategic alliances, so we will use them as an example of how to create and manage alliance teams. In the mid-1990s, Lilly recognized that alliances with biotech companies would be critical to accessing a new pipeline of drugs. Consequently, in 1999 it established the Office of Alliance Management (OAM) and made a commitment to being the premier partner in the pharmaceutical industry.[3]

The establishment of this office helped to create the context necessary to focus on developing effective alliance teams.

During the due diligence visit to each potential partner, an OAM team member conducts a cultural assessment of the partner before the alliance is established. The team member also assigns an alliance manager to each newly formed alliance to act as an "honest broker" and help manage the complexities of the alliance relationship (the alliance manager supports the alliance leader, the Lilly person who is responsible for managing the alliance team with the partner's alliance leader on a day-to-day basis). The OAM has developed a toolkit, or set of processes, specifically designed to help manage the idiosyncratic features of alliance teams. The alliance manager's job is to become proficient with that toolkit. Thus, the leader of such a team is trained in how to manage these alliances. In the following sections we describe some of the processes that have helped Lilly become a leader in managing alliance teams.

Cultural Assessment: The Due Diligence Team

After establishing hundreds of alliances, Lilly has learned that "differences in partner cultures are the number-one reason for alliance failure."[4] As a result, after identifying potential partners, Lilly tries to assess whether they will be able to work together effectively on an interorganizational team.

Lilly has developed a process of sending a due diligence team to the potential alliance partner to do a systematic evaluation of the partner's assets, resources, and processes, and to assess the partner's culture. The team (between 2 and 20 people depending on the size and complexity of the partner) visits the potential partner for two to three days to assess the partner's financial condition, information technology, research capabilities, quality, health and safety record, and culture.

During the cultural assessment, the team examines the potential partner's corporate values and expectations, organization structure, reward systems and incentives, leadership styles and decision-making processes, human interaction patterns, work practices, history of partnerships, and human resource management practices. Lilly can identify potential areas of conflict if it can understand the following:

- Differences in corporate values, such as different priorities placed on growth, revenues, profitability, and innovation
- Differences in organization structure, such as whether the partner has a centralized or decentralized management approach
- Differences in decision-making styles, such as whether the partner values fast decision-making processes versus slower consensus-building processes or whether the partner values disagreement and debate
- Differences in leadership styles, such as whether the partner tends to rely on autocratic versus more nurturing leadership styles
- Differences in reward systems, such as whether the partner rewards high-performing employees with stock options or bonuses or promotions or bigger offices and titles

Lilly's cultural assessment helps it understand why an alliance team may fail even before it is formed. By understanding what factors may throw the team off track, it can educate team members so that they are aware of potential conflicts and can staff and govern the team in a way that will increase the probability that the team will work well together.

Strategic Futures Exercise

Once an alliance team is formed, Lilly conducts a strategic futures exercise to make sure all members of the alliance team are clear on the strategic intent of the alliance relationship. During this exercise, all team members have the opportunity to describe what they think are the key objectives of the alliance team. Each member responds to two questions:

1. What specifically are the alliance team's goals and objectives next year and three years from now?
2. How does each team member prioritize those goals?

After identifying and discussing the team's goals, the team engages in a discussion to identify what they think will be the key barriers to achieving those goals. These could be technological challenges, regulatory challenges, marketing or distribution challenges, or simply specific challenges associated with working together effectively. After identifying the key barriers, the team discusses strategies for overcoming those barriers. This discussion is critical because anticipating the barriers to goal achievement and devising some initial strategies to respond to those barriers allows the team to avoid the problems that often beset alliance teams early in the relationship. Moreover, this discussion helps the team identify the operating principles by which they are going to make the relationship work. Finally, this discussion helps build trust among team members by helping them see that they are committed to common goals.

Strategic Decision-Making Template

After completing the strategic futures exercise, Lilly's alliance teams develop a decision-making template in a two-step process to assist the team with the intricacies of shared decision making:

1. Identify the key decisions or types of decisions that the team will need to make.
2. Identify which persons or organizational unit is responsible for making each type of decision (for example, steering committee, operating committee, task team, functional pairs of individuals).

The team usually starts by identifying the most important and challenging decisions and then works down to the less critical decisions. It then typically assigns responsibility for making those decisions to the co-chairs of one of the alliance team's three (sometimes more) decision-making units or a functional pair of individuals. Each alliance team has at least these three decision-making units: steering committee, operating committee, and task team. There should be clarity regarding who signs off on changes in the project budget or allocation of funds; who makes decisions about licensing jointly developed intellectual property; who makes decisions about product pricing; who decides on the wording, content, and timing of press releases; and so on:

The steering committee is the highest-level decision-making body and typically comprises senior executives from both organizations. This committee signs off on the most critical strategic decisions, such as the project budget, capital investments, deployment of intellectual property, and the product development plan.

The operating committee, a step below the steering committee, comprises senior managers from both sides who are involved in the day-to-day activities of the alliance. It typically is charged with making resource allocation and personnel decisions and approves specific work plans for the team.

Task teams typically are sub-teams within the larger alliance team that are charged with performing specific tasks, such as developing the manufacturing, marketing, or distribution plans, or working with government bodies to get regulatory approval.

Finally, within the alliance team, Lilly typically forms functional pairs, or individuals within the same function from both organizations who must make specific decisions about development, marketing, distribution, manufacturing, finance, and so on. This team composition ensures that each party has its key functional areas represented.

It is often the case that the alliance team will form a functional pair in marketing and give primary responsibility for key marketing activities to an individual at one of the partner organizations (the "lead"). This individual may then develop plans to target specific decision makers with a particular marketing pitch through particular media. However, before making the final decisions about the marketing plan, the individual must get the input and sign-off on these decisions from his or her "functional pair" from the partner organization. This is important because the functional pair understands how marketing is done at the partner organization and will know whether the marketing plan is consistent with that company's processes and values. Disagreements on decisions between functional pairs often are elevated to a task team or operating committee level. Similarly, key disagreements at the operating committee level typically will be addressed by the steering committee. This process creates clarity regarding who should make certain decisions and how to handle disagreements.

In addition to creating a decision-making template, Lilly's alliance team develops a communication and work planning document that (1) identifies each major task that the team needs to perform; (2) for each task, identifies who is responsible for the doing the work, who is accountable for the end product, and who needs to be consulted or informed once the work is completed (Lilly refers to this as the "RACI process"); and (3) outlines the primary methods of communication, including the frequency of communication, among those who are responsible, accountable, or need to be consulted or informed.

After going through the RACI process for each task, the team discusses and agrees on how and what kind of information they are going to share with each other. This is a practical way of deciding when to use e-mail, voice mail, videoconference, electronic data interchange, and face-to-face meetings. Their goal is to make communication within the alliance team as open and transparent as possible. However, there is also the need for a common understanding of what kind of information or technology is proprietary to a particular partner organization and will not be shared. This helps identify the boundaries of what information can, and cannot, be shared within the alliance team.

Keeping the Alliance Team on Track: Annual Health Check

Lilly does regular team building on its alliance teams through a process it calls the "annual health check." It has developed a proprietary survey to check the health of its alliance teams on an annual basis. The annual heath check survey provides an understanding of how the alliance team is performing in terms of fit. There are three types of fit that Lilly looks at:

Strategic fit between partners, including commitment of the partners, alignment of the partners' objectives, and relationship qualities such as trust and fairness;

Operational fit, including attributes of effective organization and management, leadership, communication, and conflict management processes;

Cultural fit, including compatible values and ways of working together, especially ways appropriate to a knowledge industry.

Lilly uses the health check survey to assess the relative health of its larger partnerships at a particular point in time. The survey captures the differences between the way that Lilly participants and partner participants on the alliance team view the partnership in terms of how well the team is working together to achieve common goals.

Conceptually, the health check survey evaluates the degree to which the alliance team is succeeding on the broad categories of strategic fit, operational fit, and cultural fit. It then defines 14 categories that underlie those dimensions. For strategic fit, the Lilly survey uses three categories to define the dimension: commitment, strategy, and trust and fairness. For operational fit, the survey uses eight categories: communication, conflict management, decision making, leadership, performance measurement, roles, skills and competence, and team coordination. For cultural fit, the survey uses three categories: organizational values, knowledge management, and flexibility.

To measure each dimension, the instrument asks respondents to rate their degree of agreement with specific statements or questions. For example, to measure commitment to the alliance team the survey questions focus on such things as each partner's follow-through or understanding of the importance of the alliance for both companies. To measure knowledge management, the questions probe respondents' views on each partner's knowledge sharing and use of learning practices. Finally, the survey asks a set of broad "outcome" and "satisfaction" questions to assess the extent to which respondents believe the alliance is achieving its goals and objectives. The most useful report for Lilly is the "spider web" chart (see Figure 10.1) that graphs the findings for both Lilly and the partner on a circular grid. Using this graphic, Lilly and its alliance partner can easily see the categories that Lilly and the partner agree are strong, the categories both view as areas needing improvement, and categories that they evaluate differently—the gaps in perception.

Figure 10.1 Measuring Alliance Health

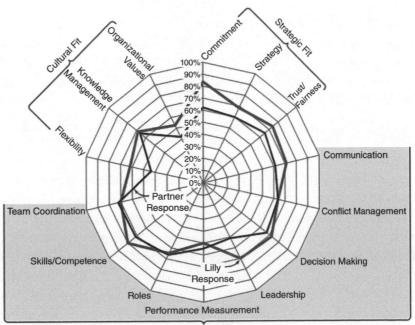

The survey is used when there are at least ten direct participants on the alliance team from both Lilly and the partner. That size ensures that the quantitative results will be meaningful. In the case of alliances with fewer than ten team members from each partner in which a large-scale survey would not be statistically meaningful, Lilly has developed a focus group process that allows the alliance manager to probe into the same issues. The initial effort was to use the survey to evaluate only Lilly's capabilities and performance as a partner, since a major purpose of the health check is to make sure Lilly is being a good partner. But in many cases, the partner requested that its capabilities and performance in the alliance be included in the survey as well. More recently, the survey has been modified so that both companies answer questions about the alliance and about the partner. The end result is the same. The survey helps pinpoint areas in which the alliance team can take steps to improve both the relationship and team performance.

Does the health check help build healthy alliance teams? Lilly claims that the health check absolutely improves alliance performance. Alliance partner respondents say that Lilly has substantially improved its ability to recognize and resolve team difficulties in the partnership at an early stage, before they become stumbling blocks. In some cases, Lilly found that it needed to replace its alliance leader. Former OAM executive director Sims said, "Through these assessments we found that we had to occasionally make some leadership changes. They were not bad leaders, just not a good fit with the particular alliance." Alliance team failure, like a failed marriage, is often the culmination of a chain of events that eventually escalates toward the collapse of the relationship. The health check allows Lilly to send in a "marriage counselor"—in this case, the alliance manager—to help get the relationship back on track before it ends in a messy divorce. In cases of significant conflict, the alliance team manager might use some of the inter-team conflict inventions described in Chapter 8 to reduce conflict between those representing the different organizations. Sometimes the health check session does not reveal any major problems but instead results in a simple improvement in the day-to-day working relationship. In other instances, the health check process directly improves project results and outcomes.

In summary, the Eli Lilly case illustrates how implementing the 5Cs can create effective alliance teams. Lilly creates the right context for their alliance teams through the OAM department, which outlines the processes to follow when creating such teams. The company is also clear about how to compose the team of functional pairs and helps the team develop competencies in setting common goals, making decisions, and engaging in open communications. Leadership training is also an important part of the process, and Lilly monitors the alliance team leaders to ensure good performance. Finally, the company is adept at managing change. They have a clear process of doing regular "health checks" concerning how the alliance is working and have clear methods for improving the relationships between partners in areas that are problematic. By paying attention to the 5Cs of team development, Eli Lilly has become an industry leader in the use of alliance teams.

Team Building in Entrepreneurial Firms

Entrepreneurship has become increasingly important to the world economy. For example, in the United States alone there are over 400,000 new businesses started each year. While we often focus on the founders of such companies like Bill Gates of Microsoft, the reality is that these start-ups are typically built and grown by small entrepreneurial teams rather than individuals. An entrepreneurial team is defined as a team that is created during or shortly after the formation of a new organization. In our experience, there are two types of entrepreneurial teams that need to be developed and managed for the entrepreneurial venture to reach its potential.

The first team is the "board of directors." Unfortunately, many entrepreneurs ignore the development and use of this type of team. Most new ventures have what we call a "paper board." This type of board exists only on paper and is usually comprised of family members and possibly the family's accountant (this is because most start-ups are family businesses). It rarely, if ever, meets formally.

The second type of board is a "rubberstamp" board. This board is also typically comprised of family members and possibly a few senior managers who work at the company. This board does meet on a regular basis, but its role is not to critique the operations of the business but merely to rubberstamp the decisions that have already been made by the company's founder (or founders). These two types of boards provide little or no value to the business as compared to an "advisory board," which we will describe in more detail shortly.

The second team needing attention in the entrepreneurial firm is the "top management team." This team is comprised of the senior managers in the organization typically representing the various functions such as sales, finance, manufacturing, and so forth. The role of this team is to develop and implement the firm's strategy in order to give it a competitive advantage in the marketplace. In particular, this type of team needs to be creative to solve problems since the new firm is trying to establish its place in the market and often needs to respond to issues and challenges that unexpectedly arise.

Challenges in Team Building in Entrepreneurial Firms

There are two main reasons why team building tends to be difficult in entrepreneurial firms. The first has to do with the leadership style of founders of such firms, and the second has to do with the fact that the board and the top management team are newly formed, with team members having little or no history together. As the firm grows, new members are usually added to each team—particularly the management team. Thus, the newness of the teams and their changing compositions present some unique challenges for team development. We will discuss both challenges in turn.

Leadership Style in Entrepreneurial Firms

There has been considerable research on entrepreneurs and their leadership style.[5] While there is variation in the kinds of leadership behaviors exhibited by entrepreneurs, there are some leadership characteristics that are quite common. Characteristics of entrepreneurs that make team building more difficult in entrepreneurial firms include:

- **Secrecy.** Entrepreneurs often keep information to themselves. This allows them to be one-up on others and provides them with a power base to influence others.

- **Need for control.** Entrepreneurs often start their firms because they want to have control over their lives and over the decisions that are made. Thus, they tend to have an authoritarian leadership ship style—"It's my way or the highway"—and are not open for suggestions or criticism.

- **Overconfidence bias.** Research shows that entrepreneurs are afflicted with a cognitive bias called the "overconfidence bias."[6] In other words, entrepreneurs are overconfident that their judgments are correct. This can be a good thing for starting a business because the entrepreneur will stay persistent in pursuing the venture even when others may not believe in the venture (of course, it can also cause an entrepreneur to pursue a new venture even when it becomes clear that it will not be successful). However, when a firm leader is overconfident in his or her judgments this can create challenges for collaborative decision making and inclusion.

- **Poor delegation.** If entrepreneurial founders have both a need for control and the overconfidence bias, then this can lead to an inability to effectively delegate. Entrepreneurs, when they do delegate, may not be willing to delegate meaningful assignments, and often don't have the time or patience to follow up with those to whom they delegate assignments.

- **Lack of interest in team building.** Entrepreneurs tend to have a bias for action. Thus, they may see spending time on team development activities as a waste of time. Since entrepreneurs often see themselves as putting out many "fires" as they launch their businesses, they don't feel they can spend time or resources to focus on teamwork.

These five characteristics of entrepreneurs can make team building a challenge in an entrepreneurial organization. However, if team members are selected carefully for both their skills to contribute to the new venture and their belief in the new venture's mission, then start-up teams can collaborate effectively even with the challenges listed above. The following strategies for developing effective boards of directors and top management teams have the characteristics of entrepreneurs in mind in the design of a team-building program.

Using the 5Cs in the Entrepreneurial Firm

We have found our 5C model especially applicable to entrepreneurial firms and we have consulted with founders to create effective boards and top management teams. We will examine each C in turn for both a board of directors and the top management team.

Team Context Creating the right context is very important for having a well-functioning board of directors. Having this context begins when the founders create their initial founding documents—articles of incorporation (for C and S corporations) and articles of organization (for limited liability corporations). These documents should stipulate who should be on the board of directors. In some cases, the founders may want to create an "advisory" board for the firm rather than have a formal board of directors. (This may need to be the case in a partnership agreement. Sole proprietors might also want to have an advisory board as well.) The documents should outline how many people should be on the board (we recommend at least three in a start-up organization) with at least two of the board members coming from outside of the company. The articles should list how many times the board should meet each year (at least four but maybe more times depending on the need). Compensation for board members should be outlined as well. Board members need to be elected by the shareholders each year, typically with a maximum term of three years. This allows new blood to be on the board to give the board new ideas and reinvigorate the board. These guidelines provide the context for having an effective board.

In the case of the top management team, there should be a basic "memorandum of understanding" on how this team should function, although this memo need not be part of the articles of incorporation. The memo of understanding should outline which managers (or managerial roles) should be on the top management team, how often the team should meet, the kinds of decisions that should be made by the team, and what authority team members should have. We have found that some entrepreneurs we have worked with are uncomfortable in a team setting, preferring to interact with their subordinates one-on-one. However, these entrepreneurs make it difficult to unleash the power that can be developed in their team. Thus, putting in writing how often a team should meet and other guidelines helps to clarify expectations about how the team should function and encourages the entrepreneur to focus on the team.

Composition The composition of the board is important to its success as the governing body for a start-up. The board should typically have at least two outside representatives. The outsiders should have business experience related to the potential problems facing the business—particularly the problem of how to grow the business successfully. Moreover, outside board members should have experience and expertise that the founder(s) does not have. Board members who have had broad experience in managing a similar company and have gone through the growing pains that will likely be experienced by the business are usually the best board members. Individuals with narrow technical expertise are best to be involved as consultants to the organization, rather than as board members. The board should meet quarterly, or more often if necessary. Board members are typically paid a retainer for being on the board, as well as a fee for coming to a board meeting. Typical retainers for smaller start-ups would be about $2,000 with $1,000 for each board meeting. Thus, the cost per board member would be about $6,000 per year—but a lot depends on the firm's cash flow and the expectations of board members. We have found that some retired executives are willing to serve on a board for free or are paid only for their expenses related to board service. In some instances, board members are given equity (i.e. ownership) in the firm, but we have found that equity only makes sense if the board member is going to be a long-term contributor to the firm. Moreover, equity should be earned over time, typically over a three- or four-year time period.

In the case of the top management team, the team should have representatives from every area of the business that is critical for the business to grow. Having people on the team that can manage the issues external to the organization—sales, customer relations, fund raising, and so on—and others who are best at managing internal issues—engineering, manufacturing, and so on—are needed on such a team. A team member who might serve in the role of a facilitator or "devil's advocate" to help keep the team on track and make sure that the team looks at all the issues can be important for certain teams when the entrepreneur tends to dominate the discussions.

Competencies The first competency that is important for the board is meeting management since the board members devote most of their time contributing to the firm during formal board meetings. Many board meetings are run poorly and fail to help management or improve the organization. A typical board meeting lasts between four and eight hours. Before a board meeting takes place, all board members should receive information regarding the performance of the business since the previous board meeting. An agenda for the board meeting should also be included. The agenda should cover the following items:

- **A review of firm performance.** This part of the board meeting should take only an hour or so.
- **A review of the key problems facing the business and what to do about them.** This item should take the bulk of the time in the board meeting.
- **A review of future company plans**—expansion, new products, and so on—and getting feedback from the board.

- **Developing a plan of action.** The board should outline the steps that need to be taken to solve the problems of the company. Often board members will have assignments to help solve the organization's problems. Effective boards also have basic performance appraisals for board members (which could even consist of having each board member provide a brief assessment each year of the value he or she has brought to the company).

Running an effective board meeting is essential to get the most out of the board. Once board meetings are operating effectively, the other key competencies have to do with the team being able to communicate openly and honestly (having outsiders usually facilitates this, but this competency should be discussed openly by the board). The role of the board is typically not to make decisions for the organization, but to advise the founder(s) on how solve important business problems and to provide insight to help the firm grow. In most instances, the founder(s) have control of the firm's ownership so they can fire board members at will. Thus, an advisory role makes the most sense for those outsiders on the board. However, if firm owners on the board have a disagreement, then a vote may need to be taken, and in such cases the outsiders can wield significant power in decision making.

Competencies in meeting management are also important for the top management team since the founder(s) may not have skills in meeting management and may not be used to meeting with such a team on a regular basis. Other needed competencies include:

- Goal setting
- Building trust
- Making assignments clear and clarifying roles
- Holding people accountable for their performance
- Open communications
- Decision making

In an entrepreneurial team, the team may experience a leadership style by the founder(s) that may make it difficult for the team to function effectively. Thus, building trust and creating open communications are essential along with setting goals, making clear assignments, and holding people accountable. Decision making can be particularly problematic given that the founder(s) may want to make many decisions by themselves that affect the entire team. The entrepreneurial team might begin its work by focusing on how to build these competencies into the team as we have outlined in Chapter 4.

Change For the board, an annual stop-start-continue activity at a board meeting would be helpful to ensure that the board is functioning properly and meeting its goals. Another option is to have an outside consultant versed in group processes attend a board meeting, and then give the board feedback on how it's functioning at the end of the meeting.

In the case of the top management team, an initial "appreciative inquiry" exercise can be helpful as a team starts its work to understand what characteristics team members believe should be part of this new team. Over time, a start-stop-continue activity or a force field analysis might also be useful to identify areas of concern and improve the team. Given that roles often shift in an entrepreneurial team, we encourage periodic role-clarification meetings, at least every six months, and more often if new people are added to the team. This allows new members to identify their roles more quickly and to understand to whom to go for help and support.

Collaborative Leadership In the case of an entrepreneurial team, the team leader is, by definition, a person who founded or co-founded the organization and has control of the firm's ownership. Thus, the leader is not likely to be replaced even if he or she is performing poorly. One option to help such leaders is to encourage them to join an organization such as the Young Presidents Organization (YPO) or other networking organization where founders can get some input and training regarding their leadership role. Having an outside team member, possibly a consultant, coach, or someone who understands group processes, meet with the team and give the team feedback on how it's functioning can also prove helpful.

Creating a Board of Directors: The Case of Acme Corporation

Several years ago we were asked to consult with a company that we will call the Acme Corporation. This organization was led by a father and his two sons, Jack and Larry. We were asked to help this family team develop a plan for leadership succession in the business. However, as we began working with this client it became apparent that they needed help in more areas than just succession planning. The company's strategy and structure needed fine tuning. Manufacturing was a bottleneck for the company. And there were significant human resource issues that required attention. To help the family deal with these concerns we recommended that they create a board of directors—the three family members were the only designated board members at the time.

To create this board, we identified some characteristics of potential board members: they should have knowledge of the industry, understand what it's like to be in a family business, and have significant experience in running a company. After generating these criteria, the family identified two outside CEOs of family owned business in the same industry (but not competitors) who they felt could serve on the board. They also wanted someone who was able to help them with succession planning so Gibb was asked to serve on the board as well. Thus, the newly constituted board had six members—three inside family members and three outsiders.

The board was tasked with meeting each quarter to help the company improve its operations. In one of our first meetings we reviewed the company's financials, which were sent to us several weeks before the meeting. The outside board members then asked a simple question: "What is your company's legal form?" The reply was: "We're a C corporation." Then we had a discussion of the tax implications of that legal form and the outside board members suggested that they change the company's legal status from a

(*Continued*)

C corporation to an S corporation to reduce their tax liability. (C corporations are taxed at both the corporate tax rate and then the profits and distributed to shareholders who are then taxed at the individual tax rate—hence double taxation. S corporation profits are only taxed at the individual tax rate after they are distributed to shareholders.) This change was made in the company's legal status and immediately the family began to receive a greater return—the board had already demonstrated its worth.

Over several years the board helped the family create more efficient manufacturing processes, helped the firm weather a layoff, and provided guidance related to managing succession. Sales and profits doubled as the board played an active role in guiding management decisions. We have seen similar results in other entrepreneurial firms where boards of directors were created using the pattern we've just described.

The Family Team

Over the years we have had the opportunity to work with many families who own and manage family businesses. Thus, we work with two teams: the family team and the business team. While there are generally overlapping members of both teams, the family team has some unique characteristics that make it a good candidate for team building. While we are not family therapists, and deep-seated problems that are a function of abuse or other traumatic events are in the domain of family therapy, there are certain issues and conflicts in families that can be resolved by using team-building techniques in a family setting. In this section we will discuss how our 5C framework can be used to help family teams. Composition, however, will not be discussed since you cannot choose who will be in your family. We're stuck with who happens to be our parents, siblings, grandparents, and extended family. But by understanding the family context, competencies needed, the type of leadership in the family that is appropriate, and using certain change strategies, families—whether in business together or not—can be helped and strengthened.

Family Context

Context for a family refers to the family members, their history together, and their relationships with one another. When working with families who operate family businesses, we start the process of understanding the context for the family by creating a "family genogram."[7] Figure 10.2 shows how the various types of relationships are depicted in the genogram.

Figure 10.2 Reading a Genogram

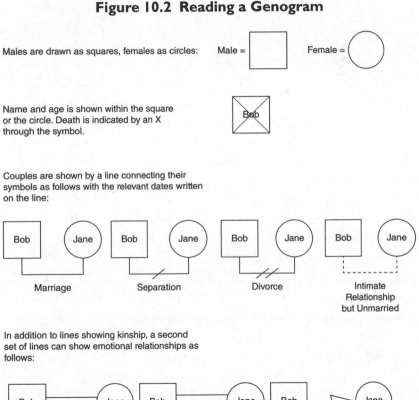

Males are drawn as squares, females as circles: Male =   Female =

Name and age is shown within the square or the circle. Death is indicated by an X through the symbol.

Bob

Couples are shown by a line connecting their symbols as follows with the relevant dates written on the line:

Bob Jane   Bob Jane   Bob Jane   Bob Jane

Marriage   Separation   Divorce   Intimate Relationship but Unmarried

In addition to lines showing kinship, a second set of lines can show emotional relationships as follows:

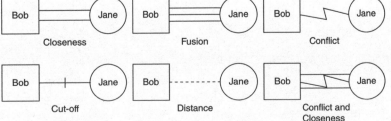

Bob Jane   Bob Jane   Bob Jane

Closeness   Fusion   Conflict

Bob Jane   Bob Jane   Bob Jane

Cut-off   Distance   Conflict and Closeness

Figure 10.3 Wilson Family Genogram

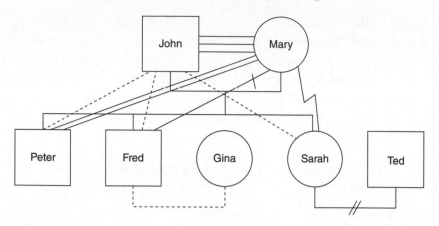

Men are depicted by squares and women by circles with the oldest children from left to right. In Figure 10.3 is an example of the "Wilson family" genogram. This genogram shows the family led by John and Mary Wilson who are married and who have a "fused" relationship, meaning that they are very close and do everything together. John, however, has a distant relationship with his three children and noted by the dashed lines while Mary has a close relationship with Peter, but has a conflictual relationship with Sarah (due to her divorce from Ted) and is cut off from Fred (meaning she doesn't have contact with Fred) because Fred is cohabiting with Gina and she disapproves of this relationship.

With a few exceptions we find that most families, when interviewed, can create a genogram that most can agree with. By creating such a genogram, the consultant or family member who wants to improve the family can determine whether or not therapy or team building would be the right approach. With some of our clients it's been both—family members are in therapy at the same time we're doing team development with the family.

Competencies

Almost every competency listed in Chapter 4 is needed to create an effective family team. For example:

- Families need to be able to set goals (e.g. financial, education, relationships, etc.) to help the family improve.
- Building trust and having open communications are essential for families to work together to achieve their goals.
- The ability of the family to make decisions together so they can be carried out with commitment is also important.
- Family members need to understand what responsibilities they have in the family (e.g. chores, making a budget, doing laundry, shopping, etc.). Much conflict in a family is the result of family members disagreeing about their roles and responsibilities.
- While not as formal as a business meeting, family members need to learn how to "meet" effectively. Family decisions and assignments should be recorded to avoid misunderstandings and to help family members follow through with their assignments.

Unfortunately, many families don't have particularly good role models to follow from their previous family experiences. Thus, we, as consultants, often find ourselves in the role of educators to help the family recognize and understand these principles. We also often spend significant time with family members to facilitate decision making and other family processes to remind the family of these competencies. We model for the family how these competencies should play out as family members interact with one another. While a consultant or facilitator can help the family develop these competencies, family members need to be committed themselves to identifying those competencies that are needed and be willing to put together a program to help the family develop them. From our experience, we have found that outside help is often necessary for certain families.

Change in the Family

During our years of teaching at various universities about organizations and teams, one assignment that we have given is to have students do a team-building project. Students are encouraged to help a team where they currently serve as a member. At times, some students have asked if they could do a team-building project with their spouses or partners and we have agreed since we've seen team-building efforts help families in our consulting practice. The typical approach used by families (with our students it's mostly couples) in doing team building is to use the stop-start-continue exercise. In reporting the results back to us, some of the common items are:

Start

- Eating dinner together in the evening
- Creating a budget for us to follow each month
- Working out together to improve our health
- Going on regular dates

Stop

- Playing too many video games
- Staying up too late at night (we need to go to bed at a reasonable hour)
- Criticizing one another when something goes wrong (think before we say something)
- Spending money on things we can't afford

Continue

- Visiting other family members on a regular basis
- Sharing how our day went with each other at the end of the day
- Going over the week's calendar on Sunday so we'll know what obligations we have during the week
- Supporting each other in our schooling and career goals

After generating these items, the family puts together an action plan to improve relationships and achieve its goals.

In the context of a family who owns a business, the role-clarification exercise can be especially helpful since family and business roles can be blurred and at times confusing to other family members since some family members may play a dual role in the family and the business. The role-clarification exercise should proceed as outlined in Chapter 8, but should be expanded so each family member can describe his or her role (or obligations) in the family and in the business (if they work in the business). Family members can then give the person input regarding those roles, negotiations that are needed can take place, and adjustments made so that family members can feel that they are supported and also understand what they should do to help others in the family succeed.

While team building may be seen as only an activity for those who work in formal organizations, the most important organization that most people will belong to is their family. We've found that the principles for team building can be applied to one's family to strengthen family relationships and help the family achieve its goals. Using the change strategies discussed above have made a difference in the families that we've worked with and can make a difference in your family as well. However, as noted previously, in cases where a family is having significant problems that are rooted in the history of family relationships, a family therapist is generally needed.

Leadership

Leadership is an interesting challenge for those in a family. When children are young, the father and mother typically serve as the leaders and the children are largely dependent, relying on the parents to make decisions for them. As the children mature, we often find relationships between the parents and teenagers becoming counter-dependent, meaning that they are often in conflict with one another. This is a natural process as children eventually want to assert their own independence and make their own decisions. In healthy families, this counter-dependent relationship eventually evolves into an interdependent relationship, where both parents and children learn how to make joint decisions and rely on each other for support. Some parents have difficulty moving out of the role of the leader who gets to make all the decisions. Such a pattern can lead to significant conflicts within the family. Thus, much like the changing nature of the leadership style of a team leader described in Chapter 6, family leaders need to learn how to share power and decision-making authority with younger family members. While children are young, they will naturally defer to their parents in decision making, but as they mature a more collaborative decision-making process is needed in the family.

Notes

1. P. Kale, J. H. Dyer, and H. Singh, "Alliance Capability, Stock Market Response, and Long-Term Alliance Success: The Role of the Alliance Function," *Strategic Management Journal* 23 (2002): 747–767.
2. PricewaterhouseCoopers study reported in Exhibit 2 of N. Sims, R. Harrison, and A. Gueth, "Managing Alliances at Lilly," *In Vivo: The Business and Medicine Report*, June 2001.
3. We thank numerous members of the Office of Alliance Management (OAM) at Eli Lilly and Company for providing insights into how Lilly manages its alliances teams. This section draws heavily on interviews with Gary Stach and Nelson Sims, current and past executive directors of OAM, and Michael Ransom and Dave Haase, current and past managers of OAM, as well as the following publications by individuals from OAM: Nelson Sims, Roger Harrison, and Anton Gueth, "Managing Alliances at Lilly," *In Vivo: The Business and Medicine Report*, June 2001; and David Futrell, Marlene Slugay, and Carol H. Stephens, "Becoming a Premier Partner: Measuring, Managing and Changing Partnering Capabilities at Eli Lilly and Company," *Journal of Commercial Biotechnology*, 8 (Summer 2001): 5–13.

4. Interview with OAM executive director Nelson Sims, October 2000.
5. W. Gibb Dyer, *The Entrepreneurial Experience* (San Francisco: Jossey-Bass, 1992).
6. L. Busenitz and J. B. Barney, "Differences Between Entrepreneurs and Managers in Large Organizations: Biases and Heuristics in Strategic Decision Making," *Journal of Business Venturing* 12 (1997): 9–30.
7. J. Hilburt-Davis and W. G. Dyer, *Consulting to Family Businesses* (San Francisco: Jossey-Bass/Pfeiffer, 2003).

11

CREATING A TEAM-BUILDING ORGANIZATION

In the introduction we described how social scientists of the 1950s started experimenting with T-groups and how this intervention evolved over time to become team building. In team building, intact workgroups, typically those facing problems, were given the tools and training to improve their performance. Unfortunately, team building is still seen by some organizations as a one-off activity: an intervention that some teams in the organization may need when they are in trouble. Few organizations have systematic programs to improve teamwork. We believe that all teams, regardless of how well they are performing, need periodic checkups to assess how they are doing and to make course corrections to continually improve. This requires more than just calling in a consultant or human resource person to work with teams periodically. It requires a *team-building organization* designed with the 5Cs in mind to create the right context, composition, competencies, change management skills, and collaborative leadership to achieve continuous improvement in team performance.

We've described several organizations in this book, such as Bain & Company, which has come a long way to becoming a team-building organization. However, one organization, Cisco Systems, seems to stand out as an excellent example of how team development can be embedded in an organization's structures, systems, and processes. Here's how Cisco Systems has built an organization-wide capability centered on an effective and ongoing team-building organization.

Cisco Systems: A Team-Building Organization[1]

Cisco Systems is a multinational organization based in the United States and is known for being the largest networking company in the world. Cisco was founded in 1984 by Leonard Bosack and Sandy Lerner, two computer scientists from Stanford University looking for a simpler way to connect different types of computer systems.[2] Cisco gained its name as a shortened version of San Francisco, and on its logo the lines represent the two towers on the Golden Gate Bridge.[3] Cisco develops, manufactures, and sells networking hardware, telecommunications equipment, and other IT services and products. These are used by service providers as well as corporations, government agencies, utilities, and education institutions. Cisco has over 70,000 employees in more than 300 locations and 115 countries. To put Cisco's impact in the industry into perspective, 85 percent of all Internet traffic travels across Cisco's systems.[4] In 2017, Cisco placed #48 in Forbes's "100 Best Places to Work" list and had $48 billion in revenue that same year.[5]

When Chuck Robbins became CEO in 2015, there was a need to shift the company's focus to recurring sales rather than fighting for traditional hardware sales—like routers or switches—which are installed once and do not need to be upgraded for several years. Thus, Robbins began to transform Cisco by making moves such as eliminating business lines that were not adding recurring revenue. As mentioned previously, 85 percent of Internet traffic travels across Cisco's network equipment, so Robbins asked the question, "Why not focus on the security of that network?" By moving into this new market, Cisco has become the largest security company in the world. In addition, Robbins and his leadership team came up with the idea to pair subscriptions with their hardware services, which dramatically increased the percentage of their revenue coming from guaranteed sources year over year instead of having to rely solely on new sales. In a nutshell, Cisco's transformation was to restructure the business to offer products and services in a way that they could generate recurring revenue.

But Cisco's transformation was not limited to its strategy and product lines. A key step to creating effective change was team alignment and team performance. When Robbins entered the organization as CEO, he identified certain organizational changes that would enable teams to be more successful, such as combining the sales and marketing departments so that they could work more closely together. This allowed these new teams to listen more carefully to their customers and ensure that they used the full complement of Cisco's products, not only to make it difficult for customers to switch to another provider, but also to make the customer experience better. There was also organizational restructuring to ensure each team had clear lines of authority for reporting, which made collaboration between teams easier. With this brief introduction, we will now use our 5C framework to discuss how Cisco has become a team-building organization.

Creating the Context for Team Success at Cisco

Francine Katsoudasi, the chief people officer of Cisco, decided that in order to have more effective teams, she needed to bring in a different perspective from someone on the outside and eventually hired Ashley Goodall, as the head of their Leadership and Team Intelligence department. He completely changed the way Cisco looked at performance management and brought to the company the best practices from Deloitte, which mostly revolved around focusing on team rather than individual performance. However, Goodall did not know what team excellence looked like at Cisco. Through his work with Marcus Buckingham, Gallup, and other organizations, he knew what generally made the best teams, but to get data about Cisco's teams he conducted the "Best Team" study at Cisco. The Best Team study conducted at Cisco identified the best team in the organization and pinpointed the keys to its success and how that success might be duplicated in other teams across the organization. The results of the study helped Goodall and Cisco articulate some of the core values that define teamwork in the organization. Two of the more important values are:

> **Win Together:** We work smart and collaborate *effectively across teams to do extraordinary things*. We're passionate about ensuring customers' and partners' success and generating profitable growth for shareholders.
>
> **Respect and Care for Each Other:** We work, grow, learn, and have fun together. We support and trust one another through change. We inspire each other, celebrate diversity of thought, encourage openness, and *reward for team results*.

These values are highlighted by corporate leaders and engrained in employees as they are taught how they do their work at Cisco.

Furthermore, with the rise of virtual teams and open office floor-plans, Cisco has also pushed for putting additional collaboration and teamwork strategies in place. Cisco's answer to problems has been to use collaboration technology, which the company produces and uses internally. Cisco's collaboration platforms do more than just create easy ways to share ideas—they help complement workflows and seamlessly support various work styles and devices. Cisco Webex Teams and Cisco Webex Meetings are just two examples of products Cisco produces which the organization uses internally. On September 20, 2018, Cisco launched a livestream called "Cisco's Collaboration Day" where company executives talked about the latest in videoconferencing, team collaboration platforms, security, and other intuitive collaboration technologies.[6] Cisco is proud of its products that support teams and the company has extensive blog articles on how to use them in the organization and how their products can be leveraged in other organizations to improve teamwork. The blog currently has almost 100 results when searching for "teamwork," demonstrating how important it is to the organization as well as company customers.

Cisco has what is known as the "People Deal," which includes a three-part promise to their employees: (1) Connect Everything,

(2) Innovate Everywhere, and (3) Benefit Everyone. In *Connect Everything*, the company expresses the desire to have a team versus individual culture, relentlessly focused on the customer. Cisco specifically mentions that teams are "with the strengths of the individuals in mind . . . creating the best teams using the strengths of those team members. Cisco promises employees to provide them with the resources, tools and direction to make that happen."[7] The third part, *Benefit Everyone*, means that Cisco invests in its employees' development and encourages them to positively impact the world, and expects in return that employees embody the company's values as they "win together."

Composition

Cisco's leadership was recently interviewed by the Great Place to Work Institute. One of the questions was: "What key characteristics tell you a prospective employee will be a great fit for your company?" Cisco's response was telling: "We're on the lookout for people who create and harness the power of teams. [People] who are just as focused on their own success as their team's success. [People] who bring diversity of thought and character to teams. We want the team builders."[8] It is clear right from the start that teams are in mind when it comes to hiring the right people at Cisco.

There are two types of teams at Cisco: permanent and temporary. The majority of teams at Cisco are permanent teams while only a handful are temporary, meaning the team members are taken from permanent teams in order to accomplish a specific objective fulfilling a business need. The temporary teams are also known as dynamic or "blast teams," and the purpose of their creation starts with two questions: "What are we trying to accomplish? And, whom do we need to involve?" For example, in an engineering initiative, there was a blast team created of about 20 team members, each from a different function at Cisco, in order to accomplish the task at hand. Blast teams are sometimes put together during the hiring process whenever there is a need to add an additional person to the team.

Getting hired at Cisco depends on many factors. A Cisco-sponsored webinar series helps job applicants prepare for the hiring process by highlighting the fact that Cisco is a place that changes often and requires adaptation and flexibility.[9] The typical time frame from the initial interview to getting hired is about three weeks,[10] and when ranked against 13 other technology companies, Cisco ranks in the top three for providing applicants with a positive experience.[11] Depending on how technical the position is there are three kinds of interviews:[12] a phone screen interview, competence-based interviews, and panel interviews led by human resource staff and hiring managers. Based on the webinar series mentioned previously, there are also other methods used to screen applicants depending on the position. These include: individual one-on-one interviews through Webex (a Cisco product) or Skype, panel or group interviews, and even working sessions to demonstrate knowledge and skill. Cisco also has a university recruiting program which uses an internship experience for college students lasting from 2 to 12 months. The program helps Cisco find the highest performers across undergraduate and graduate programs and helps the student interns think differently and see complex problems in a new light.[13]

When recruiting managers describe what traits and soft skills they want in new Cisco team members, their answers have similar themes. Across the board, verbal and written communication skills with customers and team members is a requirement. Ramon, a general manager in Mexico, notes that he looks for skills such as "conflict resolution," "influencing others," and "leadership." Leadership, broadly defined, means being outspoken about your ideas but being open to others' ideas as well. Other managers mention traits such as "resourcefulness," "high attention to detail," and "taking initiative" as essential skills, as well as their "passion for the company" along with their set of skills. It is clear that at Cisco, hiring the right person for the team is paramount, which includes not only the right skillset, but also the right blend of motivation and aligned values with the company.

Competencies

Ashley Goodall and his colleague Marcus Buckingham wrote a book called *Nine Lies About Work: A Freethinking Leader's Guide to the Real World*, which was influenced by Goodall's experience as a Cisco executive.[14] The book focuses on the strengths and cohesiveness of teams. Cisco aligns with the philosophies derived from its thought leaders, Goodall and Buckingham, which include the idea that "one size fits one" and that the power in individual uniqueness is key to a healthy organization. Freethinking leaders and innovative teams championing actions based on real-world evidence are encouraged.

The Best Team Study The Leadership and Intelligence department set out to discover the levers that drive the best outcomes in leader and team performance. To start, they identified eight questions that fell into two areas, the team (We) and the individual (Me), and four themes: Purpose, Excellence, Support, and Strengths. These eight questions are listed below.

Team (We) Questions
1. I am really enthusiastic about the mission of my company. (Purpose)
2. In my team I am surrounded by those who share my values. (Excellence)
3. My teammates have my back. (Support)
4. I have great confidence in my company's future. (Strengths)

Individual (Me) Questions
1. At work I understand what is expected of me. (Purpose)
2. I have the chance to use my strengths every day at work. (Excellence)
3. I know I will be recognized for excellent work. (Support)
4. In my work, I am always challenged to grow. (Strengths)

The researchers used these questions to analyze the top performing teams at Cisco and then, as a control group, reached out to other teams that were representative of Cisco and asked the same questions.

The theme of "purpose" focuses on why employees choose to work at Cisco, whether they understand what is expected of them, and how they feel about the mission of the company. "Excellence" is important because Cisco believes employees are motivated when team members share values and when individuals have the ability to succeed at work. "Support" is also critical for team members at Cisco. They want to know: "Do my teammates have my back?" Cisco employees often refer to Patrick Lencioni, the author of *The Ideal Team Player 2016*, who discusses the importance of "predictive trust," and "vulnerability trust" on a team.[15] Predictive trust is based on experience and history and answers the question: "Can I rely on my team to perform?" Vulnerability trust means that asking for help will not bring negative consequences, mistakes are not career ending, and that I feel safe on the team. Being able to express yourself openly without the feeling of being judged is key. "Strengths" is the fourth theme. It focuses on helping employees see a positive future for themselves at Cisco and believing they have a chance to grow and develop their talents, thereby helping to keep employees motivated and committed to stay at Cisco.

The results of Cisco's Best Team study identified the following rank ordering of the four themes for those teams that were high performing:

1. Support or Trust: "My teammates have my back."
2. Strengths: "I have an opportunity to leverage my strengths at work."
3. Excellence: "I am surrounded by those who share my values."
4. Purpose: "I am enthusiastic about the company's mission."

A workshop was designed to support the themes from this research called the "Power of Teams." The competencies of trust, personal development, shared values, and purpose are emphasized in the workshop. These competencies are then leveraged to organically develop other competencies in the team (e.g. conflict management).

After attending a Power of Teams workshop, team leaders have the option to participate in a monthly or quarterly assessment that measures the "engagement level" of each team member. There are also "check-ins" that leaders do weekly to help team members align their priorities and receive help from their manager. Marcus Buckingham also has an assessment that is provided to Cisco employees to assist in helping them identify their strengths. These are all part of what are called "rituals," the last stage of the Power of Teams workshop.

Changing Through the Power of Teams Workshop The Power of Teams workshop helps the different functions at Cisco create effective teams and strong leaders. While there are common denominators for effective teams, Cisco sees every team and leader as unique, adhering to the "one size fits one" philosophy. The Leader and Team Intelligence department helps each team and team leader define what excellence is for their team, and then the team is guided to improve in order to achieve their goals. Cisco documents and keeps a record for any team that goes through the workshop to help them own their success and be accountable for the goals and rituals formed during the workshop.

Once team members have defined what is important to their success, they then decide how they are going to behave as a team and what values they will share. They must clearly define those behaviors and values with a great level of detail, because accountability may look different to different team members. Once everyone on the team is clear about team values, business outcomes become the focus.

One unique aspect of this workshop is a series of activities that allow each team member to share details about his or her personal life. For example, team members are asked to respond to the series of questions: "What is going well in your life? What is not? What are the challenges you are working on? Anything you're afraid of in and out of the workplace? Can your team help you?" The work at Cisco is challenging, especially in the context of Cisco's transformation, the demands are high, and team members need help to achieve their goals. Team members must rely on each other as they try to adapt the many changes occurring at Cisco, and developing this vulnerable trust is key to their success. It is important for team members to share personal information to foster an environment of trust and to assume some degree of vulnerability with other team members. The theory is: if you understand your team members on a personal level, you will have their backs, which is a key component of a successful team at Cisco. Team members can also see that their leaders are vulnerable. Thus, the workshop activities humanize them and demonstrate that even successful team leaders can struggle at times.

The workshop agenda has three simple steps. First, the team defines what excellence is to them. Second, the team goes through exercises to get to know each other on a personal level in order to learn each other's strengths and build trust. The final part of the workshop is rituals. Rituals concern an agreement of how team members and leaders will hold each other accountable. Also, human resource business partners assigned to the team keep track of these rituals and provide coaching for team leaders. The Power of Teams workshop has been completed by a pilot group and presented to all the teams. The leaders who have gone through the workshop are sharing their success stories with their peers and they're even asking for more training to improve their teams.

Results of the Workshop Teams report that by addressing these important team development issues, they can do their work more effectively. They no longer walk on eggshells when it comes to conflict since they have an environment of openness and trust. Meetings where people leave wondering if the decisions made were good ideas are a thing of the past. Teams report that the right decisions get made more quickly and meetings become more meaningful and efficient.

More engaged team members are also a result of the workshop. Individuals who previously wanted to leave Cisco now want to stay.

Collaborative Leadership

Leadership is as important as the team itself for Cisco, hence the department's name: "Leadership and Team Intelligence." One section of the department is wholly focused on improving leadership. This part of the department helps leaders to drive the team outcomes of purpose, excellence, support, and strengths. Leaders are not forced to accept the department's help—participation is voluntary. But because leaders and teams within Cisco are hungry for team development and change management skills, leaders generally want to avail themselves of the department's resources. The fundamental motivation to improve is a business necessity—in such a competitive industry they must continually improve. Human resource business partners in every branch of the organization are looking to help teams and team leaders better meet their business needs and recommend resources to help them. It is important for the leaders and their teams to buy into and personally own the process of improvement.

Servant-based leadership, where leaders are seen as a resource or helper for team members rather than as "the boss," is another prevalent mindset at Cisco that makes reaching team outcomes possible. One question Cisco answers in choosing a team leader is: Does this person have the "passion" and "skills" to accomplish the goals that are set for the team? Employees are expected to decline to lead a project if they know they are not motivated or do not have the necessary skills to complete the project successfully.

What We Can Learn from the Cisco Case?

The Cisco Case provides us with many examples of how the company paid attention to the Five Cs and how they were integrated into the organization to create a successful team building organization.

Using our 5C framework, here are some of the key actions taken by Cisco executives to emphasize the importance of teams:

Context

1. Cisco's CEO, Chuck Robbins, linked the importance of team development to the organization's new strategy of developing recurrent streams of income. As Cisco employees saw that new team dynamics were important to the implementation of the new strategy, they were more motivated to implement the new program. Efforts to improve team performance that are disconnected from an organization's mission and strategy are likely to fail since team members won't see the relevance of the team-building efforts.

2. The company explicitly states the importance of teamwork in its values statements.

3. The company explicitly rewards team performance.

4. A department was created to specifically focus on improving team performance through leadership training and team development activities.

5. Physical space in the company was designed to encourage people to meet as a team.

6. Cisco uses its technologies to allow virtual teams to communicate effectively and do their work.

7. The company encourages the use of blast or temporary teams to solve important organizational problems. This approach again emphasizes why teams are needed at Cisco.

8. On a regular basis the company assesses the engagement level of its employees.

Composition

1. Cisco has a clear profile of those potential employees who will be successful at the company. People need to be team-oriented, have the requisite skills, take initiative, and be able to adapt easily to a changing environment.

2. Furthermore, Cisco clearly articulates these attributes in a webinar that prospective employees can view and study even before going through the recruiting process. This gives potential employees a realistic job preview and helps orient them to Cisco.

3. The company has a well-developed internship program that provides a pool of potential candidates and allows the company to assess their abilities before they are hired.

Competencies

1. Cisco has gone to extraordinary lengths to articulate the competencies and values that are needed for individuals and teams to succeed. The company's Best Team study helped to identify these characteristics and employees can read about these concepts in books and blogs written by Cisco managers and their affiliates.

2. The Power of Teams workshop teaches and solidifies these principles in Cisco employees and Cisco teams. Teaching important principles like "trust," "support," and "openness" creates a foundation for effective team performance. Moreover, the workshops are just not a one-time activity. Team leaders are encouraged to have their teams participate in team workshops on a regular basis.

3. Human resource managers are assigned to each team to follow up on the workshop activities and help the team apply them to their everyday work activities.

Change

1. During the workshop the team determines its goals and how to achieve them.

2. The team uses the experience from the workshop to problem-solve and come up with ways to improve its performance. Data generated about the team is used as part of this process.

3. Improving trust in the team through sharing personal experiences is leveraged to build better relationships that can help teams when change is difficult.

4. The results of these activities have been more involved and committed employees, better decision making in the team, and better team performance.

Collaborative Leadership

1. Cisco's leadership understands the characteristics of effective team leaders and looks for leaders with the passion and skills to lead their teams. The Leadership and Team Intelligence department helps provide the leadership framework and training to help Cisco's team leaders.

2. Team leaders are encouraged to collaborate with others in the organization to avail their team of the resources needed to improve team performance. This could be in the form of the workshops provided by Cisco, the support provided by human resources, or several other alternatives.

3. Cisco's team leaders are encouraged to take a "servant-leader" role where they are tasked with helping their team members succeed. This role is particularly important in highly mature teams where facilitation by the leader rather than authoritarian leadership is needed.

Applying Cisco's Strategies in Your Organization

These are just some of the characteristics of Cisco Systems' team development activities that have led to high performance by their teams. What is clear about the Cisco case is: CISCO *takes teams seriously*. While all organizations are different, and Cisco clearly has more resources than most organizations, all organizations can take steps to improve the performance of their teams. By creating a team-building organization, team development activities become routine as part of "what we do" at our company and this leads to a process of continuous improvement. Your organization may not have the resources to create a department to focus strictly on teams, but you might be able to assign some employees to be "team resource" individuals. These individuals could help teams gather data about themselves to improve their performance, organize regular workshops on team development, and modify many context variables, such as team rewards, to encourage teams to perform better. While our 5C model and the interventions that we describe in previous chapters can be very helpful for individual teams, infusing one's organization with a team-building culture will pay dividends that are larger and more consistent than if team building is done only when a team is in trouble.

Conclusion

In this book we've given you the tools that you need to help your team be more effective. Use the 5C framework to identify which of the Cs are causing problems for your team and require attention. Then choose an intervention or interventions that are applicable to your problems and try them. If you don't feel you have the skills within the team to facilitate the intervention, then ask for help from those with experience facilitating team building. Continue to track your progress and performance (e.g. through personal management interviews or regular team meetings) and make course corrections if needed. Finally, start the process of becoming a team-building organization to ensure that team development and team performance are a consistent priority in your organization.

This process is not easy. But teamwork is the key to solving the complex problems our world faces. Moreover, being part of an effective team is important to our success and well-being as individuals. As Michael Jordan, perhaps the greatest individual basketball player of our time, once said: "Talent wins games, but teamwork and intelligence win championships." In most situations the difference between success and failure is a great team.

Notes

1. The case and chapter were written with the help of Natalia Smith.
2. https://www.cisco.com/c/en_au/about/who-is-head.html.
3. https://en.wikipedia.org/wiki/Cisco_Systems.
4. https://www.cisco.com/c/en_au/about/who-is-head.html.
5. https://www.statista.com/topics/2286/cisco/.
6. https://blogs.cisco.com/collaboration/collaboration-day.
7. https://www.forbes.com/sites/patrickmoorhead/2018/08/08/ciscos-people-deal-exemplifies-its-cutting-edge-commitment-to-employees/.
8. http://reviews.greatplacetowork.com/cisco.
9. bit.ly/JobAtCisco.
10. https://www.indeed.com/cmp/Cisco/faq/hiring-process.
11. https://www.huffingtonpost.com/reuben-yonatan/which-tech-companies-have_b_8991840.html.
12. https://www.cisco.com/c/en/us/about/careers/working-at-cisco/students-and-new-graduate-programs/interview-tips.html.
13. http://research.cisco.com/students.
14. Buckingham and A. Goodall. (2019). Nine Lies About Work: A Freethinking Leader's Guide to the Real World. Boston: Harvard Business Review Press.
15. P. Lencioni, The Ideal Team Player (Hoboken, NJ: Wiley, 2016).

Index